Quick & Easy
Low Fat

Contents

Introduction

Healthy eating means that you can enjoy all of your favorite foods and still keep in great shape. These carefully selected recipes will show you how you can eat nutritious, filling, well-balanced meals, full of flavor and low in fat. Packed full of dishes that are quick and simple to prepare, *Low Fat* provides an array of healthy, low-fat dishes for you, your family and your guests to enjoy.

Reducing Your Fat Intake

Reducing the fat content in our diet is very easy, and the benefits are myriad. Not only do supermarkets provide a variety of healthy alternatives to full-fat ingredients, such as reduced-fat dairy products, but the variety of fresh fruit and vegetables available provides excellent sources of essential vitamins. The easiest and quickest way to reduce your fat calorie intake is to change from full-fat milk, cream, cheese and yoghurt to a low- or reduced-fat equivalent. Semi-skimmed milk, for example, has all the nutritional benefits of whole milk but $^1/_3$ oz of fat per pint compared with $^3/_4$ oz of fat per pint in whole milk.

The Benefits of Fat

Reducing the level of fat in your diet is synonymous with losing weight. Yet there are many benefits in eating the right types of fat of which many dieters are unaware. It is important to remember that we all need to include a certain amount of fat in our daily intake to function properly. Essential fatty acids are required in order to build cell membranes and for other vital bodily functions. Our brain tissues, nerve sheaths and bone marrow need fat, and we also need fat to protect our organs such as our liver, kidneys and heart.

When is Fat Bad?

Fat is bad when we consume a high level of it in our diet. Too much fat increases the risk of developing coronary disease, diabetes and even cancer — and, of course, it can lead to obesity. But high-fat diet-related illnesses are not limited to those who are overweight.

Nutritionists suggest that we should aim to cut our intake of fat to 27—30 per cent of our total daily calorie intake. If your average diet totals 2000 calories, this will mean eating no more than about $2^3/_4$ oz of fat a day. As a guide, most people consume 40 per cent of their daily calories in the form of fat. However, you should always consult your family doctor if you are being treated for any medical condition before you begin a new regime.

Different Types of Fat

Fats are made up of a combination of fatty acids and glycerol. Fatty acids consist of a chain of carbon atoms linked to hydrogen atoms. The way these are linked determines whether they are saturated or unsaturated fats, and consequently if they should be avoided or not.

Saturated fats. These are easily recognizable. Saturated fats are solid at room temperature and are mainly found in animal products, such as meat and dairy foods, although some vegetable oils, including palm and coconut oil, contain them.

Our body has difficulty processing these saturated fats and, as a result, it tends to store them. They increase cholesterol levels in the bloodstream, which can in turn increase the risk of heart disease. It is therefore important to reduce the level of saturated fats in the diet: they should comprise no more than 30 per cent of the total fat intake or no more than nine per cent of the total energy intake.

Unsaturated fats. These are normally liquid or soft at room temperature and are thought to reduce the level of cholesterol in the bloodstream. There are two types of unsaturated fats: monounsaturated and polyunsaturated. The former are mainly found in veg-etables, but they also occur in oily fish, such as mackerel. The latter are only found in oily fish and seed oils.

Cooking Methods

The way we cook our food is one of the most important factors in ensuring a healthy, low-fat diet. In general, steaming is the best way to cook vegetables to preserve their goodness. Boiling can, for example, destroy up to three-quarters of the vitamin C present in green vegetables. This guide will help you to choose the healthiest way to cook your dish, while maintaining optimum flavor and color.

KEY

🍞 Simplicity level 1 – 3 (1 easiest, 3 slightly harder)

🥘 Preparation time

🕐 Cooking time

- **Frying**. This is the most fat-rich method of cooking. Yet, surprisingly, deep-frying the food absorbs less fat than shallow-frying. To cut down on fat intake, buy a good quality, non-stick skillet as you will need less fat, and use a vegetable oil, high in polyunsaturates. A good method is to stir-fry food: you require little oil as the food is cooked quickly over a high heat.

- **Broiling**. This is a good alternative to frying, producing a crisp, golden coating whilst keeping food tender and moist. Ingredients with a delicate texture and which can easily dry out, such as white fish or chicken breasts, will require brushing with oil. Marinating can reduce the need for oil. Always cook on a rack, so that the fat drains away.

- **Poaching**. This is ideal for foods with a delicate texture or subtle flavor, such as chicken and fish, and it is fat free. The cooking liquid can make the basis of a nutri-tious and flavorsome sauce: try alternative liquids such as stock, wine and acidulated water, flavored with herbs and vegetables.

- **Steaming**. This is also fat-free and is becoming a popular method of cooking meat, fish, chicken and vegetables. Ingredients maintain their color, flavor and texture, fewer nutrients are leached out. An additional advantage is that when meat is steamed, the fat melts and drips into the cooking liquid – this should not then be used for gravy.

- **Braising and stewing**. Slow-cooking techniques produce succulent dishes that are especially welcome in winter. Trim all visible fat from the meat and always remove the skin from the chicken.

- **Roasting**. Fat is an integral part of this cooking tech-nique and without it meat or fish would dry out. Try standing meat on a rack over a roasting tray so that the fat drains off. Do not use the meat juices for gravy.

- **Baking**. Many dishes are fat free. Foil-wrapped parcels of meat or fish are always delicious. Add fruit juice or wine instead of oil or butter for a moist texture.

- **Microwave**. Food cooked in this way rarely requires additional fat.

Chicken & Leek Soup

This satisfying soup can be served as a main course. You can add rice and bell peppers to make it even more hearty, as well as colorful.

NUTRITIONAL INFORMATION

Calories	183	Sugar	.........4g
Protein	........21g	Fats	..........9g
Carbohydrates	....4g	Saturates	......5g

5 MINS   1¼ HOURS

SERVES 4–6

INGREDIENTS

2 tbsp butter

12 oz boneless chicken

12 oz leeks, cut into 1-inch pieces

5 cups chicken stock

1 bouquet garni sachet

8 pitted prunes, halved

salt and white pepper

cooked rice and diced bell peppers
   (optional)

1 Melt the butter in a large saucepan.

2 Add the chicken and leeks to the saucepan and fry for 8 minutes.

3 Add the chicken stock and bouquet garni sachet and stir well.

4 Season well with salt and pepper to taste.

5 Bring the soup to the boil and simmer for 45 minutes.

6 Add the prunes to the saucepan with some cooked rice and diced bell peppers (if using) and simmer for about 20 minutes.

7 Remove the bouquet garni sachet from the soup and discard. Serve the chicken and leek soup immediately.

VARIATION

Instead of the bouquet garni sachet, you can use a bunch of fresh mixed herbs, tied together with string. Choose herbs such as parsley, thyme and rosemary.

Beef Soup with Rice

Strips of tender lean beef are combined with crisp water chestnuts and cooked rice in a tasty beef broth with a tang of orange.

NUTRITIONAL INFORMATION

Calories	.210	Sugar	.4g
Protein	.20g	Fats	.5g
Carbohydrates	...21g	Saturates	...2g

25 MINS   25 MINS

SERVES 4

INGREDIENTS

12 oz lean beef (such as rump or sirloin)

1 quart beef stock

1 cinnamon stick, broken

2 star anise

2 tbsp dark soy sauce

2 tbsp dry sherry

3 tbsp tomato paste

4 oz can water chestnuts, drained and sliced

3 cups cooked white rice

1 tsp zested orange rind

6 tbsp orange juice

salt and pepper

TO GARNISH

strips of orange rind

2 tbsp chives, snipped

1 Carefully trim away any fat from the beef. Cut the beef into thin strips and then place into a large saucepan.

2 Pour over the stock and add the cinnamon, star anise, soy sauce, sherry, tomato paste and water chestnuts. Bring to the boil, skimming away any surface scum with a flat ladle. Cover the pan and simmer gently for about 20 minutes.

3 Skim the soup with a flat ladle to remove any more scum. Remove and discard the cinnamon and star anise and blot the surface with absorbent kitchen paper to remove any fat.

4 Stir in the rice, orange rind and juice. Check the seasoning. Heat through for 2–3 minutes before ladling into warm bowls. Serve garnished with strips of orange rind and snipped chives.

COOK'S TIP

Omit the rice for a lighter soup that is an ideal starter for an Oriental meal of many courses. For a more substantial soup that would be a meal in its own right, add diced vegetables such as carrot, bell pepper, corn or zucchini.

Italian Platter

This popular hors d'oeuvre usually consists of vegetables soaked in olive oil and rich, creamy cheeses. Try this great low-fat version.

NUTRITIONAL INFORMATION

Calories 198	Sugars 12g
Protein 12g	Fat 6g
Carbohydrate ...25g	Saturates 3g

🍴 10 MINS   🕐 0 MINS

SERVES 4

INGREDIENTS

4½ oz reduced-fat Mozzarella cheese, drained

2 oz lean prosciutto

14 oz can artichoke hearts, drained

4 ripe figs

1 small mango

few plain bread sticks, to serve

DRESSING

1 small orange

1 tbsp sieved tomatoes

1 tsp wholegrain mustard

4 tbsp low-fat unsweetened yogurt

fresh basil leaves

salt and pepper

VARIATION

For a change, serve with a French stick or an Italian bread, widely available from supermarkets, and use to mop up the delicious dressing.

1 Cut the cheese into 12 sticks, 2½ inches long. Remove the fat from the ham and slice the meat into 12 strips. Carefully wrap a strip of ham around each stick of cheese and arrange neatly on a serving platter.

2 Halve the artichoke hearts and cut the figs into quarters. Arrange them on the serving platter in groups.

3 Peel the mango, then slice it down each side of the large, flat central stone. Slice the flesh into strips and arrange them so that they form a fan shape on the serving platter.

4 To make the dressing, pare the rind from half of the orange using a vegetable peeler. Cut the rind into small strips and place them in a bowl. Extract the juice from the orange and add it to the bowl containing the rind.

5 Add the strained tomatoes, mustard, yogurt and seasoning to the bowl and mix together. Shred the basil leaves and mix them into the dressing.

6 Spoon the dressing into a small dish and serve with the Italian Platter, accompanied with bread sticks.

Parsley, Chicken & Ham Pâté

Pâté is easy to make at home, and this combination of lean chicken and ham mixed with herbs is especially straightforward.

NUTRITIONAL INFORMATION

Calories	119	Sugars	.........2g
Protein	........20g	Fat	...........3g
Carbohydrate	....2g	Saturates	......1g

55 MINS | 0 MINS

SERVES 4

INGREDIENTS

8 oz lean, skinless chicken, cooked

3½ oz lean ham, trimmed

small bunch fresh parsley

1 tsp lime rind, grated

2 tbsp lime juice

1 garlic clove, peeled

½ cup low-fat unsweetened yogurt

salt and pepper

1 tsp lime zest, to garnish

TO SERVE

wedges of lime

crisp bread

green salad

VARIATION

This pâté can be made successfully with other kinds of minced, lean, cooked meat such as turkey, beef and pork. Alternatively, replace the meat with peeled shrimp and/or white crab meat, or with canned tuna in brine, drained.

1 Dice the chicken and ham and place in a blender or food processor.

2 Add the parsley, lime rind and juice, and garlic to the chicken and ham, and process well until finely minced. Alternatively, finely chop the chicken, ham, parsley and garlic and place in a bowl. Mix gently with the lime rind and juice.

3 Transfer the mixture to a bowl and mix in the yogurt. Season with salt and pepper to taste, cover and leave to chill in the refrigerator for about 30 minutes.

4 Pile the pâté into individual serving dishes and garnish with lime zest. Serve the pâtés with lime wedges, crisp bread and a fresh green salad.

Minted Onion Bhajis

Gram flour (also known as besan flour) is a fine yellow flour made from garbanzo beans and is available from supermarkets and Asian food stores.

NUTRITIONAL INFORMATION

Calories 251	Sugars 7g	
Protein 7g	Fat 8g	
Carbohydrate . . .39g	Saturates 1g	

5 MINS   15 MINS

MAKES 12

I N G R E D I E N T S

1 cup gram flour

¼ tsp cayenne pepper

¼–½ tsp ground cilantro

¼–½ tsp ground cumin

1 tbsp chopped fresh mint

4 tbsp strained thick low-fat yogurt

¼ cup cold water

1 large onion, quartered and thinly sliced

vegetable oil, for frying

salt and pepper

sprigs of mint, to garnish

1 Put the gram flour into a bowl, add the cayenne pepper, cilantro, cumin and mint and season with salt and pepper to taste. Stir in the yogurt, water and sliced onion and mix well together.

2 One-third fill a large, deep skillet with oil and heat until very hot. Drop heaped spoonfuls of the mixture, a few at a time, into the hot oil and use two forks to neaten the mixture into rough ball-shapes.

3 Fry the bhajis until golden brown and cooked through, turning frequently.

4 Drain the bhajis on absorbent paper towels and keep warm while cooking the remainder in the same way.

5 Arrange the bhajis on a platter and garnish with sprigs of fresh mint. Serve hot or warm.

COOK'S TIP

Gram flour is excellent for making batter and is used in India in place of flour. It can be made from ground split peas as well as garbanzo beans.

Vegetables with Tahini Dip

This tasty dip is great for livening-up simply-cooked vegetables.
You can vary the vegetables according to the season.

NUTRITIONAL INFORMATION

Calories 126   Sugars 7g
Protein ....11g   Fat 6g
Carbohydrate ....8g   Saturates 1g

5 MINS   20 MINS

SERVES 4

INGREDIENTS

8 oz small broccoli florets

8 oz small cauliflower florets

8 oz asparagus, sliced into
    2 inch lengths

2 small red onions, quartered

1 tbsp lime juice

2 tsp toasted sesame seeds

1 tbsp chopped fresh chives, to garnish

HOT TAHINI &
GARLIC DIP

1 tsp sunflower oil

2 garlic cloves, crushed

½–1 tsp chili powder

2 tsp tahini (sesame seed paste)

⅔ cup low-fat unsweetened yogurt

2 tbsp chopped fresh chives

salt and pepper

1 Line the base of a steamer with baking parchment and arrange the vegetables on top.

2 Bring a wok or large saucepan of water to the boil, and place the steamer on top. Sprinkle with lime juice and steam for 10 minutes.

3 To make the hot tahini & garlic dip, heat the sunflower oil in a small non-stick saucepan, add the garlic, chili powder and seasoning to taste and fry gently for 2–3 minutes until the garlic is softened.

4 Remove the saucepan from the heat and stir in the tahini (sesame seed paste) and yogurt. Return to the heat and cook gently for 1–2 minutes without boiling. Stir in the chives.

5 Remove the vegetables from the steamer and place on a warmed serving platter. Sprinkle with the sesame seeds and garnish with chopped chives. Serve with the hot dip.

Bruschetta

Traditionally, this Italian savory is enriched with olive oil. Here, sun-dried tomatoes are a good substitute and only a little oil is used.

NUTRITIONAL INFORMATION

Calories	178	Sugars	.........2g
Protein	.........8g	Fat	...........6g
Carbohydrate	...24g	Saturates	......2g

45 MINS   5 MINS

SERVES 4

I N G R E D I E N T S

¼ cup dry-pack sun-dried tomatoes

1¼ cups boiling water

14 inch long Granary or whole wheat stick of French bread

1 large garlic clove, halved

¼ cup pitted black olives in brine, drained and quartered

2 tsp olive oil

2 tbsp chopped fresh basil

⅓ cup grated low-fat Italian Mozzarella cheese

salt and pepper

fresh basil leaves, to garnish

1 Place the sun-dried tomatoes in a heatproof bowl and pour over the boiling water.

2 Set aside for 30 minutes to soften. Drain well and pat dry with paper towels. Slice into thin strips and set aside.

3 Trim and discard the ends from the bread and cut into 12 slices. Arrange on a broiler rack and place under a preheated hot broiler and cook for 1–2 minutes on each side until lightly golden.

4 Rub both sides of each piece of bread with the cut sides of the garlic. Top with strips of sun-dried tomato and olives.

5 Brush lightly with olive oil and season well. Sprinkle with the basil and Mozzarella cheese and return to the broiler for 1–2 minutes until the cheese is melted and bubbling.

6 Transfer to a warmed serving platter and garnish with fresh basil leaves.

COOK'S TIP

If you use sun-dried tomatoes packed in oil, drain them, rinse well in warm water and drain again on paper towels to remove as much oil as possible.
Sun-dried tomatoes give a rich, full flavor to this dish, but thinly-sliced fresh tomatoes can be used instead.

Cheesy Ham Savory

Lean ham wrapped around crisp celery, topped with a light crust of cheese and scallions, makes a delicious light lunch.

NUTRITIONAL INFORMATION

Calories 188	Sugars 5g	
Protein 15g	Fat 12g	
Carbohydrate 5g	Saturates 7g	

10 MINS   10 MINS

SERVES 4

INGREDIENTS

4 sticks celery, with leaves

12 thin slices of lean ham

1 bunch scallions

6 oz low-fat soft cheese with garlic and herbs

6 tbsp low-fat unsweetened yogurt

4 tbsp Parmesan cheese, freshly grated

celery salt and pepper

TO SERVE

tomato salad

crusty bread

1 Wash the celery, remove the leaves and reserve (if wished). Slice each celery stick into 3 equal portions.

2 Cut any visible fat off the ham and lay the slices on a chopping board. Place a piece of celery on each piece of ham and roll up. Place 3 ham and celery rolls in each of 4 small, heatproof dishes.

3 Trim the scallions, then finely shred both the white and green parts. Sprinkle the scallions over the ham and celery rolls and season with celery salt and pepper.

4 Mix the soft cheese and yogurt and spoon over the ham and celery rolls.

5 Preheat the broiler to medium. Sprinkle each portion with 1 tbsp grated Parmesan cheese and broil for 6–7 minutes until hot and the cheese has formed a crust. If the cheese starts to brown too quickly, lower the broiler setting slightly.

6 Garnish with celery leaves (if using) and serve with a tomato salad and crusty bread.

COOK'S TIP

Parmesan is useful in low-fat recipes because its intense flavor means you need to use only a small amount.

Spicy Garbanzo Bean Snack

You can use fresh garbanzo beans, soaked overnight, for this popular Indian snack, but the canned variety is just as flavorsome.

NUTRITIONAL INFORMATION

Calories 190	Sugars 4g	
Protein 9g	Fat 3g	
Carbohydrate ...34g	Saturates 0.3g	

5 MINS   10 MINS

SERVES 4

INGREDIENTS

14 oz can garbanzo beans, drained

2 medium potatoes

1 medium onion

2 tbsp tamarind paste

6 tbsp water

1 tsp chili powder

2 tsp sugar

1 tsp salt

TO GARNISH

1 tomato, sliced

2 fresh green chilies, chopped

fresh cilantro leaves

1 Place the garbanzo beans in a bowl.

COOK'S TIP

Garbanzo beans have a nutty flavor and slightly crunchy texture. Indian cooks also grind these to make a flour called gram or besan, which is used to make breads, thicken sauces, and to make batters for deep-fried dishes.

2 Using a sharp knife, cut the potatoes into dice.

3 Place the potatoes in a saucepan of water and boil until cooked through. Test by inserting the tip of a knife into the potatoes – they should feel soft and tender. Set the potatoes aside.

4 Using a sharp knife, finely chop the onion. Set aside until required.

5 Mix together the tamarind paste and water. Add the chili powder, sugar and salt and mix again. Pour the mixture over the garbanzo beans.

6 Add the onion and the diced potatoes, and stir to mix. Season to taste.

7 Transfer to a serving bowl and garnish with tomatoes, chilies and cilantro leaves.

Crêpes with Curried Crab

Home-made crêpes are delicious – here, white crab meat is lightly flavored with curry spices and tossed in a low-fat dressing.

NUTRITIONAL INFORMATION

Calories	279	Sugars	.........9g
Protein	........25g	Fat	...........7g
Carbohydrate	...31g	Saturates	......1g

40 MINS   25 MINS

SERVES 4

I N G R E D I E N T S

4 oz buckwheat flour

1 large egg, beaten

1¼ cups skimmed milk

4½ oz frozen spinach, thawed, well-drained and chopped

2 tsp vegetable oil

FILLING

12 oz white crab meat

1 tsp mild curry powder

1 tbsp mango chutney

1 tbsp reduced-calorie mayonnaise

2 tbsp low-fat unsweetened yogurt

2 tbsp fresh cilantro, chopped

TO SERVE

green salad

lemon wedges

1 Sift the flour into a bowl and remove any husks that remain in the strainer. Make a well in the centre of the flour and add the egg. Whisk in the milk, then blend in the spinach. Transfer to a jug and leave for 30 minutes.

2 To make the filling, mix together all the ingredients, except the cilantro, in a bowl, cover and chill until required. Whisk the batter. Brush a small crêpe pan with a little oil, heat until hot and pour in enough batter to cover the base thinly. Cook for 1–2 minutes, turn over and cook for 1 minute until golden. Repeat to make 8 pancakes, layering them on a plate with baking parchment.

3 Stir the cilantro into the crab mixture. Fold each pancake into quarters. Open one fold and fill with the crab mixture. Serve warm, with a green salad and lemon wedges.

VARIATION

Try lean diced chicken in a light white sauce or peeled shrimp instead of the crab.

Cranberry Turkey Burgers

This recipe is bound to be popular with children and is easy to prepare for their supper.

NUTRITIONAL INFORMATION

Calories 209	Sugars 15g
Protein 22g	Fat 5g
Carbohydrate . . .21g	Saturates 1g

🕝 🕝

🍲 45 MINS   🕐 25 MINS

SERVES 4

I N G R E D I E N T S

1½ cups lean ground turkey

1 onion, chopped finely

1 tbsp chopped fresh sage

6 tbsp dry white breadcrumbs

4 tbsp cranberry sauce

1 egg white, size 2, lightly beaten

2 tsp sunflower oil

salt and pepper

T O   S E R V E

4 toasted granary or whole wheat burger buns

½ lettuce, shredded

4 tomatoes, sliced

4 tsp cranberry sauce

1 Mix together the turkey, onion, sage, seasoning, breadcrumbs and cranberry sauce, then bind with egg white.

2 Press into 4 x 4 inch rounds, about ¾ inch thick. Chill the burgers for 30 minutes.

3 Line a broiler rack with baking parchment, making sure the ends are secured underneath the rack to ensure they don't catch fire. Place the burgers on top and brush lightly with oil. Put under a preheated moderate broiler and cook for 10 minutes. Turn the burgers over, brush again with oil. Cook for a further 12–15 minutes until cooked through.

4 Fill the burger rolls with lettuce, tomato and a burger, and top with cranberry sauce.

COOK'S TIP

Look out for a variety of ready ground meats at your butchers or supermarket. If unavailable, you can grind your own by choosing lean cuts and processing them in a blender or food processor.

Stuffed Mushrooms

Large mushrooms have more flavor than the smaller button mushrooms. Serve these mushrooms as a side vegetable or appetizer.

NUTRITIONAL INFORMATION

Calories ....148 Sugars 1g
Protein ....11g Fat 7g
Carbohydrate ....11g Saturates 3g

10 MINS   15 MINS

SERVES 4

INGREDIENTS

12 open-cap mushrooms

4 scallions, chopped

4 tsp olive oil

3½ oz fresh brown breadcrumbs

1 tsp fresh oregano, chopped

3½ oz low-fat sharp
   Cheddar cheese

1 Wash the mushrooms and pat dry with paper towels. Remove the stalks and chop the stalks finely.

2 Sauté the mushroom stalks and scallions in half of the oil.

3 In a large bowl, mix together the mushroom stalks and scallions.

4 Add the breadcrumbs and oregano to the mushrooms and scallions, mix and set aside.

5 Crumble the cheese into small pieces in a small bowl. Add the cheese to the breadcrumb mixture and mix well. Spoon the stuffing mixture into the mushroom caps.

6 Drizzle the remaining oil over the mushrooms. Grill on an oiled rack over medium hot coals for 10 minutes or until cooked through.

7 Transfer the mushrooms to serving plates and serve hot.

VARIATION

For a change replace the cheese with finely-chopped chorizo sausage (remove the skin first), chopped hard-boiled eggs, chopped olives or chopped anchovy fillets. Mop up the juices with some crusty bread.

Pasta Provençale

A combination of Italian vegetables tossed in a tomato dressing, served on a bed of assorted salad leaves, makes an appetizing meal.

NUTRITIONAL INFORMATION

Calories	197	Sugars	.........5g
Protein	........10g	Fat	...........5g
Carbohydrate	...30g	Saturates	......1g

10 MINS   15 MINS

SERVES 4

INGREDIENTS

8 oz quills

1 tbsp olive oil

1 oz pitted black olives, drained and chopped

1 oz dry-pack sun-dried tomatoes, soaked, drained and chopped

14 oz can artichoke hearts, drained and halved

4 oz baby zucchini, trimmed and sliced

4 oz baby plum tomatoes, halved

3½ oz assorted baby salad leaves

salt and pepper

shredded basil leaves, to garnish

DRESSING

4 tbsp strained tomatoes

2 tbsp low-fat unsweetened yogurt

1 tbsp unsweetened orange juice

1 small bunch fresh basil, shredded

1 Cook the quills according to the instructions on the packet. Do not overcook the pasta – it should still have 'bite'. Drain well and return to the pan.

2 Stir in the olive oil, salt and pepper, olives and sun-dried tomatoes. Leave to cool.

3 Gently mix the artichokes, zucchini and plum tomatoes into the cooked pasta. Arrange the salad leaves in a serving bowl.

4 To make the dressing, mix all the ingredients together and toss into the vegetables and pasta.

5 Spoon the mixture on top of the salad leaves and garnish with shredded basil leaves.

Lamb & Tomato Koftas

These little meatballs, served with a minty yogurt dressing, can be prepared well in advance, ready to cook when required.

NUTRITIONAL INFORMATION

Calories 183	Sugars 5g	
Protein 15g	Fat 11g	
Carbohydrate 5g	Saturates 4g	

15 MINS   10 MINS

SERVES 4

I N G R E D I E N T S

8 oz finely minced lean lamb

1½ onions, peeled

1-2 garlic cloves, peeled and crushed

1 dried red chili, finely chopped (optional)

2-3 tsp garam masala

2 tbsp chopped fresh mint

2 tsp lemon juice

salt

2 tbsp vegetable oil

4 small tomatoes, quartered

mint sprigs, to garnish

Y O G U R T   D R E S S I N G

⅔ cup low-fat yogurt

2 inch piece cucumber, grated

2 tbsp chopped fresh mint

½ tsp toasted cumin seeds (optional)

1 Place the minced lamb in a bowl. Finely chop 1 onion and add to the bowl with the garlic and chili (if using). Stir in the garam masala, mint and lemon juice and season well with salt. Mix well.

2 Divide the mixture in half, then divide each half into 10 equal portions and form each into a small ball. Roll balls in the oil to coat. Quarter the remaining onion half and separate into layers.

3 Thread 5 of the spicy meatballs, 4 tomato quarters and some of the onion layers on to each of 4 pre-soaked bamboo or metal skewers.

4 Brush the vegetables with the remaining oil and cook the koftas under a hot broiler for about 10 minutes, turning frequently until they are browned all over and cooked through.

5 Meanwhile, prepare the yogurt dressing for the koftas. In a small bowl mix together the yogurt, grated cucumber, mint and toasted cumin seeds (if using).

6 Garnish the lamb and tomato koftas with mint sprigs and place on a large serving platter. Serve the koftas hot with the yogurt dressing.

Cheese & Chive Biscuits

These classic biscuits have been given a healthy twist by the use of low-fat soft cheese and reduced-fat Cheddar cheese.

NUTRITIONAL INFORMATION

Calories 297	Sugars 3g	
Protein 13g	Fat 7g	
Carbohydrate . . .49g	Saturates 4g	

🥧 10 MINS   🕐 20 MINS

MAKES 10

I N G R E D I E N T S

8 oz self-rising flour

1 tsp powdered mustard

½ tsp cayenne pepper

½ tsp salt

3½ oz low-fat soft cheese with added herbs

2 tbsp fresh snipped chives, plus extra to garnish

3½ fl oz and 2 tbsp skimmed milk

2 oz reduced-fat sharp Cheddar cheese, grated

low-fat soft cheese, to serve

1 Preheat the oven to 200°C/400°F/Gas Mark 6. Sift the flour, mustard, cayenne and salt into a mixing bowl.

2 Add the soft cheese to the mixture and mix together until well incorporated. Stir in the snipped chives.

3 Make a well in the centre of the ingredients and gradually pour in 3½ fl oz milk, stirring as you pour, until the mixture forms a soft dough.

4 Turn the dough on to a floured surface and knead lightly. Roll out until ¾ inch thick and use a 2 inch plain pastry cutter to stamp out as many rounds as you can. Transfer the rounds to a cookie sheet.

5 Re-knead the dough trimmings together and roll out again. Stamp out more rounds – you should be able to make 10 biscuits in total.

6 Brush the biscuits with the remaining milk and sprinkle with the grated cheese. Bake in the oven for 15–20 minutes until risen and golden. Transfer to a wire rack to cool. Serve warm with low-fat soft cheese, garnished with chives.

VARIATION

For sweet biscuits, omit the mustard, cayenne pepper, chives and grated cheese. Replace the flavored soft cheese with plain low-fat soft cheese. Add 2¾ oz currants and 1 oz superfine sugar. Serve with low-fat soft cheese and fruit spread.

Oat-Crusted Chicken Pieces

A very low-fat chicken recipe with a refreshingly light, mustard-spiced sauce, which is ideal for a healthy lunchbox or a light meal with salad.

NUTRITIONAL INFORMATION

Calories 120	Sugars 3g
Protein 15g	Fat 3g
Carbohydrate 8g	Saturates 1g

🔥 5 MINS 🕐 40 MINS

SERVES 4

INGREDIENTS

⅓ cup rolled oats

1 tbsp chopped fresh rosemary

4 skinless chicken quarters

1 egg white

½ cup natural low-fat unsweetened yogurt

2 tsp wholegrain mustard

salt and pepper

grated carrot salad, to serve

1 Mix together the rolled oats, chopped fresh rosemary and salt and pepper.

2 Brush each piece of chicken evenly with egg white, then coat in the oat mixture.

3 Place the chicken pieces on a cookie sheet and bake in a preheated oven, 200°C/400°F/Gas Mark 6, for about 40 minutes. Test to see if the chicken is cooked by inserting a skewer into the thickest part of the chicken – the juices should run clear without a trace of pink.

4 Mix together the yogurt and mustard, season with salt and pepper to taste.

5 Serve the chicken, hot or cold, with the sauce and a grated carrot salad.

Hot Pot Chops

A Hot Pot is a lamb casserole, made with carrots and onions and with a potato topping. The chops used here are an interesting alternative.

NUTRITIONAL INFORMATION

Calories 250	Sugars 2g
Protein 27g	Fat 12g
Carbohydrate 8g	Saturates 5g

🥗 10 MINS   🕐 30 MINS

SERVES 4

I N G R E D I E N T S

4 lean, boneless lamb leg steaks, about 4½ oz each

1 small onion, thinly sliced

1 medium carrot, thinly sliced

1 medium potato, thinly sliced

1 tsp olive oil

1 tsp dried rosemary

salt and pepper

fresh rosemary, to garnish

freshly steamed green vegetables, to serve

1 Preheat the oven to 180°C/350°F/Gas Mark 4. Using a sharp knife, trim any excess fat from the lamb steaks.

2 Season both sides of the steaks with salt and pepper and arrange them on a cookie sheet.

3 Alternate layers of sliced onion, carrot and potato on top of each lamb steak.

4 Brush the tops of the potato lightly with oil, season well with salt and pepper to taste and then sprinkle with a little dried rosemary.

5 Bake the hot pot chops in the oven for 25–30 minutes until the lamb is tender and cooked through.

6 Drain the lamb on paper towels and transfer to a warmed serving plate.

7 Garnish with fresh rosemary and serve accompanied with a selection of green vegetables.

VARIATION

This recipe would work equally well with boneless chicken breasts. Pound the chicken slightly with a meat mallet or covered rolling pin so that the pieces are the same thickness throughout.

Kibbeh

This Lebanese grill dish is similar to the Turkish kofte and the Indian kofta, but the spices used to flavor the meat are quite different.

NUTRITIONAL INFORMATION

Calories	232	Sugars	.........3g
Protein	........19g	Fat	..........13g
Carbohydrate	....9g	Saturates	......4g

🦀 🦀

🧊 1 HOUR   🕐 15 MINS

SERVES 4

I N G R E D I E N T S

2¾ oz couscous

1 small onion

12 oz lean minced lamb

½ tsp ground cinnamon

¼ tsp cayenne

4 tsp ground allspice

green salad and onion rings, to serve

B A S T E

2 tbsp tomato catsup

2 tbsp sunflower oil

1 Place the couscous in a large bowl, cover with cold water and leave to stand for 30 minutes or until the couscous has swelled and softened. Alternatively, soak the couscous according to the instructions on the packet.

2 Drain the couscous through a strainer and squeeze out as much moisture as you can.

3 If you have a food processor, add the onion and chop finely. Add the lamb and process briefly to chop the mince further. If you do not have a processor, grate the onion then add to the lamb.

4 Combine the couscous, lamb and spices and mix well together. Divide the mixture into 8 equal sized portions. Press and shape the mixture around 8 skewers, pressing the mixture together firmly so that it holds it shape. Leave to chill for at least 30 minutes or until required.

5 To make the baste, combine the oil and catsup.

6 Grill the kibbeh over hot coals for 10–15 minutes, turning and basting frequently. Serve with grilled onion rings and green salad leaves.

Lamb with a Spice Crust

Lamb neck fillet is a tender cut that is not too thick and is, therefore, ideal for cooking on the grill.

NUTRITIONAL INFORMATION

Calories	203	Sugars	.........9g
Protein	........16g	Fat	..........10g
Carbohydrate	...12g	Saturates	......4g

5 MINS   45 MINS

SERVES 4

I N G R E D I E N T S

1 tbsp olive oil

2 tbsp light muscovado sugar

2 tbsp wholegrain mustard

1 tbsp horseradish sauce

1 tbsp all-purpose flour

12 oz neck fillet of lamb

salt and pepper

T O S E R V E

coleslaw

slices of tomato

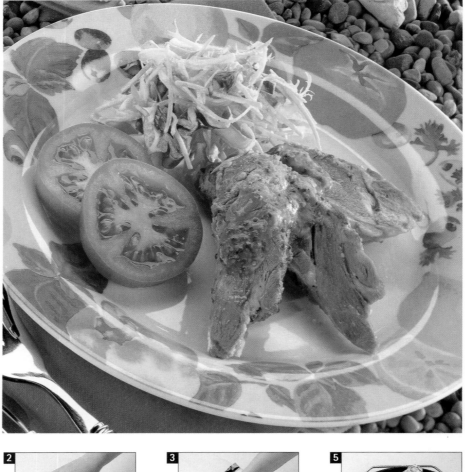

1 Combine the oil, sugar, mustard, horseradish sauce, flour and salt and pepper to taste in a shallow, non-metallic dish until they are well mixed.

2 Roll the lamb in the spice mixture until well coated.

COOK'S TIP

If preferred, the lamb can be completely removed from the kitchen foil for the second part of the cooking. Grill the lamb directly over the coals for a smokier grill flavor, basting with extra oil if necessary.

3 Lightly oil one or two pieces of foil or a large, double thickness of foil. Place the lamb on the foil and wrap it up so that the meat is completely enclosed.

4 Place the foil parcel over hot coals for 30 minutes, turning the parcel over occasionally.

5 Open the kitchen foil, spoon the cooking juices over the lamb and continue to grill for a further 10-15 minutes or until cooked through.

6 Placer the lamb on a platter and remove the foil. Cut into thick slices and serve with coleslaw and tomato slices.

Pork & Apple Skewers

Flavored with mustard and served with a mustard sauce, these kabobs make an ideal lunch.

NUTRITIONAL INFORMATION

Calories	290	Sugars	........11g
Protein	........24g	Fat	..........17g
Carbohydrate	....11g	Saturates	......5g

10 MINS   15 MINS

SERVES 4

INGREDIENTS

1 lb pork fillet

2 dessert apples

a little lemon juice

1 lemon

2 tsp wholegrain mustard

2 tsp Dijon mustard

2 tbsp apple or orange juice

2 tbsp sunflower oil

crusty brown bread, to serve

MUSTARD SAUCE

1 tbsp wholegrain mustard

1 tsp Dijon mustard

6 tbsp light cream

1 To make the mustard sauce, combine the wholegrain and Dijon mustards in a small bowl and slowly blend in the cream. Leave to stand until required.

2 Cut the pork fillet into bite-size pieces and set aside until required.

3 Core the apples, then cut them into thick wedges. Toss the apple wedges in a little lemon juice – this will prevent any discoloration. Slice the lemon.

4 Thread the pork, apple and lemon slices alternately on to 4 metal or pre-soaked wooden skewers.

5 Mix together the mustards, apple or orange juice and sunflower oil. Brush the mixture over the kabobs and grill over hot coals for 10–15 minutes, until cooked through, frequently turning and basting the kabobs with the mustard marinade.

6 Transfer the kabobs to warm serving plates and spoon over a little of the mustard sauce. Serve the kabobs with fresh, crusty brown bread.

Ginger Beef with Chili

Serve these fruity, hot and spicy steaks with noodles. Use a non-stick ridged skillet to cook with a minimum of fat.

NUTRITIONAL INFORMATION

Calories	179	Sugars	........8g
Protein	........21g	Fat	...........6g
Carbohydrate	....8g	Saturates	......2g

🌶 🌶

🍲 40 MINS   🕐 10 MINS

SERVES 4

INGREDIENTS

4 lean beef steaks (such as rump, sirloin or fillet), 3½ oz each

2 tbsp ginger wine

1 inch piece fresh ginger, finely chopped

1 garlic clove, crushed

1 tsp ground chili

1 tsp vegetable oil

salt and pepper

red chili strips, to garnish

TO SERVE

freshly cooked noodles

2 scallions, shredded

RELISH

8 oz fresh pineapple

1 small red bell pepper

1 red chili

2 tbsp light soy sauce

1 piece stem ginger in syrup, drained and chopped

1   Trim any excess fat from the beef if necessary. Using a meat mallet or covered rolling pin, pound the steaks until ½ inch thick. Season on both sides and place in a shallow dish.

2   Mix the ginger wine, fresh ginger, garlic and chili and pour over the meat. Cover and chill for 30 minutes.

3   Meanwhile, make the relish. Peel and finely chop the pineapple and place it in a bowl. Halve, deseed and finely chop the bell pepper and chili. Stir into the pineapple together with the soy sauce and ginger. Cover and chill until required.

4   Brush a broiler pan with the oil and heat until very hot. Drain the beef and add to the pan, pressing down to seal. Lower the heat and cook for 5 minutes. Turn the steaks over and cook for a further 5 minutes.

5   Drain the steaks on paper towels and transfer to serving plates. Garnish with chili strips, and serve with noodles, scallions and the relish.

Meatball Brochettes

Children will love these tasty meatballs on a skewer, which are economical and easy to make on the grill.

NUTRITIONAL INFORMATION

Calories	120	Sugars	.........2g
Protein	........17g	Fat	...........5g
Carbohydrate	....2g	Saturates	......2g

1 HOUR   10 MINS

SERVES 4

INGREDIENTS

1 oz cracked wheat

12 oz lean ground beef

1 onion, chopped very finely (optional)

1 tbsp tomato catsup

1 tbsp brown fruity sauce

1 tbsp chopped, fresh parsley

beaten egg, to bind

8 cherry tomatoes

8 button mushrooms

oil, to baste

8 bread finger rolls, to serve

1 Place the cracked wheat in a bowl and cover with boiling water. Leave to soak for 20 minutes or until softened. Drain thoroughly and leave to cool.

2 Place the soaked wheat, minced beef, onion (if using), catsup, brown fruity sauce and chopped fresh parsley together in a mixing bowl and mix well until all the ingredients are well combined. Add a little beaten egg if necessary to bind the mixture together.

3 Using your hands, shape the meat mixture into 18 even-sized balls. Leave to chill in the refrigerator for 30 minutes.

4 Thread the meatballs on to 8 pre-soaked wooden skewers, alternating them with the cherry tomatoes and button mushrooms.

5 Brush the brochettes with a little oil and grill over hot coals for about 10 minutes, until cooked through, turning occasionally and brushing with a little more oil if the meat starts to dry out.

6 Transfer the meatball brochettes to warm serving plates. Cut open the bread finger rolls and push the meat and vegetables off the skewer into the open rolls, using a fork. Serve immediately.

Pork with Ratatouille Sauce

Serve this delicious combination of meat and vegetables with baked potatoes for an appetizing supper dish.

NUTRITIONAL INFORMATION

Calories 230	Sugars 8g	
Protein 29g	Fat 9g	
Carbohydrate 8g	Saturates 3g	

🕒 10 MINS 🕒 35 MINS

SERVES 4

INGREDIENTS

4 lean, boneless pork chops, about 4½ oz each

1 tsp dried mixed herbs

salt and pepper

baked potatoes, to serve

SAUCE

1 medium onion

1 garlic clove

1 small green bell pepper, deseeded

1 small yellow bell pepper, deseeded

1 medium zucchini, trimmed

3½ oz button mushrooms

14 oz can chopped tomatoes

2 tbsp tomato paste

1 tsp dried mixed herbs

1 tsp superfine sugar

COOK'S TIP

This vegetable sauce could be served with any other broiled or baked meat or fish. It would also make an excellent alternative filling for savory crêpes.

1 To make the sauce, peel and chop the onion and garlic. Dice the bell peppers. Dice the zucchini. Wipe and halve the mushrooms.

2 Place all of the vegetables in a saucepan and stir in the chopped tomatoes and tomato paste. Add the dried herbs, sugar and plenty of seasoning. Bring to the boil, cover and simmer for 20 minutes.

3 Meanwhile, preheat the broiler to medium. Trim away any excess fat from the chops, then season on both sides and rub in the dried mixed herbs. Cook the chops for 5 minutes, then turn over and cook for a further 6–7 minutes or until cooked through.

4 Drain the chops on absorbent kitchen paper and serve accompanied with the sauce and baked potatoes.

Sweet Lamb Fillet

Lamb fillet, enhanced by a sweet and spicy glaze, is cooked on the grill in a kitchen foil parcel for deliciously moist results.

NUTRITIONAL INFORMATION

Calories	258	Sugars	........13g
Protein	........24g	Fat	..........13g
Carbohydrate	...13g	Saturates	......5g

5 MINS   1 HOUR

SERVES 4

I N G R E D I E N T S

2 fillets of neck of lean lamb, each 8 oz

1 tbsp olive oil

½ onion, chopped finely

1 clove garlic, crushed

1 inch piece fresh ginger, grated

5 tbsp apple juice

3 tbsp smooth apple sauce

1 tbsp light muscovado sugar

1 tbsp tomato catsup

½ tsp mild mustard

salt and pepper

green salad leaves, croûtons and fresh crusty bread, to serve

1 Place the lamb fillet on a large piece of double thickness kitchen foil. Season with salt and pepper to taste.

2 Heat the oil in a small pan and fry the onion and garlic for 2–3 minutes until softened but not browned. Stir in the grated ginger and cook for 1 minute, stirring occasionally.

3 Stir in the apple juice, apple sauce, sugar, catsup and mustard and bring to the boil. Boil rapidly for about 10 minutes until reduced by half. Stir the mixture occasionally so that it does not burn and stick to the base of the pan.

4 Brush half of the sauce over the lamb, then wrap up the lamb in the kitchen foil to completely enclose it. Grill the lamb parcels over hot coals for about 25 minutes, turning the parcel over occasionally.

5 Open out the kitchen foil and brush the lamb with some of the sauce. Continue to grill for a further 15–20 minutes or until cooked through.

6 Place the lamb on a chopping board, remove the foil and cut into thick slices. Transfer to serving plates and spoon over the remaining sauce. Serve with green salad leaves, croûtons and fresh crusty bread.

Fried Liver with Thyme

This elegant dish is very simple to make. You can use either calf's or lamb's liver for the main ingredient.

NUTRITIONAL INFORMATION

Calories	462	Sugars	.........1g
Protein	........27g	Fat	..........31g
Carbohydrate	...14g	Saturates	......6g

🕒 5 MINS   🕐 10 MINS

SERVES 1

INGREDIENTS

1 slice calf's liver, about 4½ oz, or
   2 smaller slices, or 2 slices lamb's liver

1 tbsp seasoned flour

2 tsp oil

1 tbsp butter or margarine

2 tbsp white wine

½ tsp chopped fresh thyme or a large pinch
   of dried thyme

pinch of finely grated lime or lemon rind

2 tsp lemon juice

1 tsp capers

1–2 tbsp heavy cream (optional)

salt and pepper

TO GARNISH

lemon or lime slices

fresh thyme or parsley

COOK'S TIP

Liver is traditionally served with bacon and onions. Broiled bacon rolls and crisply fried onions can be used as an extra garnish, if desired.

1 Trim the liver if necessary and toss in the seasoned flour until evenly coated.

2 Heat the oil and margarine in a skillet. When foaming, add the liver and fry for 2–3 minutes on each side until well sealed and just cooked through. Take care not to overcook or the liver will become tough and hard. Transfer to a plate and keep warm.

3 Add the wine, 1 tablespoon of water, the thyme, citrus rind, lemon juice, capers and seasoning to the skillet juices, and heat through gently until bubbling and syrupy. Add the cream (if using) to the sauce and reheat gently. Adjust the seasoning and spoon over the liver.

4 Serve the liver, garnished with lemon or lime slices and thyme or parsley, with new potatoes and a salad.

Minty Lamb Kabobs

These spicy lamb kabobs go well with the cool cucumber and yogurt dip. In the summer you can grill the kabobs outside.

NUTRITIONAL INFORMATION

Calories	295	Sugars	.........4g
Protein	........29g	Fat	..........18g
Carbohydrate	....4g	Saturates	......9g

5 MINS   20 MINS

SERVES 4

I N G R E D I E N T S

2 tsp cilantro seeds

2 tsp cumin seeds

3 cloves

3 green cardamom pods

6 black peppercorns

½ inch piece ginger root

2 garlic cloves

2 tbsp chopped fresh mint

1 small onion, chopped

1¾ cups ground lamb

½ tsp salt

lime slices to serve

D I P

⅔ cup low-fat natural yogurt

2 tbsp chopped fresh mint

3 inch piece of cucumber, grated

1 tsp mango chutney

1 Heat a skillet and dry-fry the cilantro, cumin, cloves, cardamom pods and peppercorns until they turn a shade darker and release a roasted aroma.

2 Grind the spices in a coffee grinder, spice mill or a pestle and mortar.

3 Put the ginger and garlic into a food processor or blender and process to a purée. Add the ground spices, mint, onion, lamb and salt and process until chopped finely. Alternatively, finely chop the garlic and ginger and mix with the ground spices and remaining kabob ingredients.

4 Mold the kabob mixture into small sausage shapes on 4 kabob skewers.

Cook under a preheated hot broiler for 10–15 minutes, turning the skewers occasionally.

5 To make the dip, mix together the yogurt, mint, cucumber and mango chutney.

6 Serve the kabobs with lime slices and the dip.

Tangy Pork Fillet

Grilled in a parcel of kitchen foil, these tasty pork fillets are served with a tangy orange sauce.

NUTRITIONAL INFORMATION

Calories	230	Sugars	........16g
Protein	........19g	Fat	...........9g
Carbohydrate	...20g	Saturates	......3g

10 MINS   55 MINS

SERVES 4

I N G R E D I E N T S

14 oz lean pork fillet

3 tbsp orange marmalade

grated rind and juice of 1 orange

1 tbsp white wine vinegar

dash of Tabasco sauce

salt and pepper

S A U C E

1 tbsp olive oil

1 small onion, chopped

1 small green bell pepper, deseeded and thinly sliced

1 tbsp cornstarch

⅔ cup orange juice

TO SERVE

cooked rice

mixed salad leaves

1 Place a large piece of double thickness foil in a shallow dish. Put the pork fillet in the centre of the foil and season.

2 Heat the marmalade, orange rind and juice, vinegar and Tabasco sauce in a small pan, stirring until the marmalade melts and the ingredients combine. Pour the mixture over the pork and wrap the meat in foil, making sure that the parcel is well sealed so that the juices cannot run out. Place over hot coals and grill for about 25 minutes, turning the parcel occasionally.

3 For the sauce, heat the oil and cook the onion for 2–3 minutes. Add the bell pepper and cook for 3–4 minutes.

4 Remove the pork from the kitchen foil and place on to the rack. Pour the juices into the pan with the sauce.

5 Grill the pork for a further 10–20 minutes, turning, until cooked through and golden on the outside..

6 In a small bowl, mix the cornstarch with a little orange juice to form a paste. Add to the sauce with the remaining cooking juices. Cook, stirring, until the sauce thickens. Slice the pork, spoon over the sauce and serve with rice and mixed salad leaves.

Teppanyaki

This simple, Japanese style of cooking, is ideal for thinly-sliced breast of chicken. You can use thin turkey escalopes, if you prefer.

NUTRITIONAL INFORMATION

Calories	206	Sugars	.........4g
Protein	........30g	Fat	..........7g
Carbohydrate	....6g	Saturates	......2g

5 MINS   10 MINS

SERVES 4

I N G R E D I E N T S

4 boneless chicken breasts

1 red bell pepper

1 green bell pepper

4 scallions

8 baby corn-on-the-cob

½ cup bean sprouts

1 tbsp sesame or sunflower oil

4 tbsp soy sauce

4 tbsp mirin

1 tbsp grated fresh ginger root

1 Remove the skin from the chicken and slice at a slight angle, to a thickness of about ¼ inch.

2 Deseed and thinly slice the bell peppers and trim and slice the scallions and corn-on-the-cob.

3 Arrange the bell peppers, scallions, corn and bean sprouts on a plate with the sliced chicken.

4 Heat a large, heavy skillet then lightly brush with oil. Add the vegetables and chicken slices in small batches, allowing space between them so that they cook thoroughly.

5 Combine the soy sauce, mirin and ginger and serve as a dip with the chicken and vegetables.

COOK'S TIP

Mirin is a rich, sweet rice wine which you can buy in oriental shops, but if it is not available add 1 tablespoon of soft light brown sugar to the sauce instead.

Karahi Chicken

A karahi is an extremely versatile two-handled metal pan, similar to a wok. Food is always cooked over a high heat in a karahi.

NUTRITIONAL INFORMATION

Calories	270	Sugars	. . . . .1g
Protein	. . . . .41g	Fat	. . . . .11g
Carbohydrate	. . . .1g	Saturates	. . . . . .2g

5 MINS   20 MINS

SERVES 4

I N G R E D I E N T S

2 tbsp ghee

3 garlic cloves, crushed

1 onion, chopped finely

2 tbsp garam masala

1 tsp cilantro seeds, ground

½ tsp dried mint

1 bay leaf

1 lb 10 oz lean boneless chicken meat, diced

scant 1 cup chicken stock

1 tbsp fresh cilantro, chopped

salt

warm naan bread or chapatis, to serve

1 Heat the ghee in a karahi, wok or a large, heavy skillet. Add the garlic and onion. Stir-fry for about 4 minutes until the onion is golden.

2 Stir in the garam masala, ground cilantro, mint and bay leaf.

3 Add the chicken and cook over a high heat, stirring occasionally, for about 5 minutes. Add the stock and simmer for 10 minutes, until the sauce has thickened

and the chicken juices run clear when the meat is tested with a sharp knife.

4 Stir in the fresh cilantro and salt to taste, mix well and serve immediately with warm naan bread or chapatis.

COOK'S TIP

Always heat a karahi or wok before you add the oil to help maintain the high temperature.

Lime Chicken Kabobs

These succulent chicken kabobs are coated in a sweet lime dressing and are served with a lime and mango relish. They make an ideal light meal.

NUTRITIONAL INFORMATION

Calories	199	Sugars	........14g
Protein	........28g	Fat	..........4g
Carbohydrate	...14g	Saturates	......1g

🖐 15 MINS   🕐 10 MINS

SERVES 4

INGREDIENTS

4 lean boneless chicken breasts, skinned, about 4½ oz each

3 tbsp lime marmalade

1 tsp white wine vinegar

½ tsp lime rind, finely grated

1 tbsp lime juice

salt and pepper

TO SERVE

lime wedges

boiled white rice, sprinkled with chili powder

SALSA

1 small mango

1 small red onion

1 tbsp lime juice

1 tbsp fresh cilantro, chopped

1 Slice the chicken breasts into thin pieces and thread on to 8 skewers so that the meat forms an S-shape down each skewer.

2 Preheat the broiler to medium. Arrange the chicken kabobs on the broiler rack. Mix together the lime marmalade, vinegar, lime rind and juice. Season with salt and pepper to taste. Brush the dressing generously over the chicken and broil for 5 minutes. Turn the chicken over, brush with the dressing again and broil for a further 4-5 minutes until the chicken is cooked through.

3 Meanwhile, prepare the salsa. Peel the mango and slice the flesh off the smooth, central stone. Dice the flesh into small pieces and place in a small bowl.

4 Peel and finely chop the onion and mix into the mango, together with the lime juice and chopped cilantro. Season, cover and chill until required.

5 Serve the chicken kabobs with the salsa, accompanied with wedges of lime and boiled rice sprinkled with chili powder.

COOK'S TIP

To prevent sticking, lightly oil metal skewers or dip bamboo skewers in water before threading the chicken on to them.

Cajun Chicken Gumbo

This complete main course is cooked in one saucepan. If you're cooking for one, halve the ingredients – the cooking time should stay the same.

NUTRITIONAL INFORMATION

Calories 425	Sugars 8g
Protein 34g	Fat 12g
Carbohydrate ...48g	Saturates 3g

🕒 5 MINS   🕐 25 MINS

SERVES 2

I N G R E D I E N T S

1 tbsp sunflower oil

4 chicken thighs

1 small onion, diced

2 stalks celery, diced

1 small green bell pepper, diced

½ cup long grain rice

1¼ cups chicken stock

1 small red chili

8 oz okra

1 tbsp tomato paste

salt and pepper

1 Heat the oil in a wide pan and fry the chicken until golden. Remove the chicken from the pan.

2 Stir in the onion, celery and pepper and fry for 1 minute. Pour off any excess oil.

3 Add the rice and fry, stirring for a further minute. Add the stock and heat until boiling. Thinly slice the chili and trim the okra. Add to the pan with the paste. Season to taste.

4 Return the chicken to the pan and stir. Cover tightly and simmer gently for 15 minutes, or until the rice is tender, the chicken is thoroughly cooked and the liquid absorbed. Stir occasionally and if it becomes too dry, add a little extra stock.

COOK'S TIP

The whole chili makes the dish hot and spicy – if you prefer a milder flavor, discard the seeds of the chili.

Citrus Duckling Skewers

The tartness of citrus fruit goes well with the rich meat of duckling.
Duckling makes a change from chicken for the grill.

NUTRITIONAL INFORMATION

Calories	205	Sugars	.........5g
Protein	........24g	Fat	..........10g
Carbohydrate	....5g	Saturates	......2g

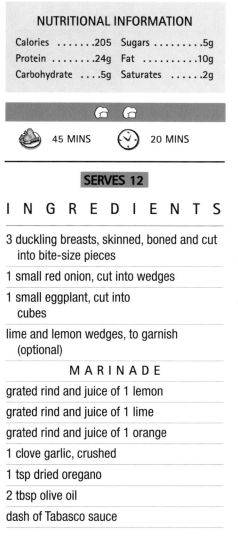

45 MINS   20 MINS

SERVES 12

I N G R E D I E N T S

3 duckling breasts, skinned, boned and cut
into bite-size pieces

1 small red onion, cut into wedges

1 small eggplant, cut into
cubes

lime and lemon wedges, to garnish
(optional)

M A R I N A D E

grated rind and juice of 1 lemon

grated rind and juice of 1 lime

grated rind and juice of 1 orange

1 clove garlic, crushed

1 tsp dried oregano

2 tbsp olive oil

dash of Tabasco sauce

1 Cut the duckling into bite-sized
pieces. Place in a non-metallic bowl
together with the prepared vegetables.

2 To make the marinade, place the
lemon, lime and orange rinds and
juices, garlic, oregano, oil and Tabasco
sauce in a screw-top jar and shake until
well combined. Pour the marinade over
the duckling and vegetables and toss to
coat. Leave to marinate for 30 minutes.

3 Remove the duckling and vegetables
from the marinade and thread them
on to skewers, reserving the marinade.

4 Grill the skewers on an oiled rack
over medium hot coals, turning and
basting frequently with the reserved
marinade, for 15-20 minutes until the
meat is cooked through. Serve the kebabs
garnished with lemon and lime wedges for
squeezing (if using).

COOK'S TIP

For more zing add 1 teaspoon of
chili sauce to the marinade. The
meat can be marinated for several
hours, but it is best to marinate the
vegetables separately for only about
30 minutes.

Chicken Jalfrezi

This is a quick and tasty way to use leftover roast chicken. The sauce can also be used for any cooked poultry, lamb or beef.

NUTRITIONAL INFORMATION

Calories	270	Sugars	.........3g
Protein	........36g	Fat	...........11g
Carbohydrate	....7g	Saturates	......2g

🦀 🦀

🍲 25 MINS   🕐 15 MINS

SERVES 4

I N G R E D I E N T S

1 tsp mustard oil

3 tbsp vegetable oil

1 large onion, chopped finely

3 garlic cloves, crushed

1 tbsp tomato paste

2 tomatoes, skinned and chopped

1 tsp ground turmeric

½ tsp cumin seeds, ground

½ tsp cilantro seeds, ground

½ tsp chili powder

½ tsp garam masala

1 tsp red wine vinegar

1 small red bell pepper, chopped

1 cup frozen fava beans

1 lb 2 oz cooked chicken, cut into bite-sized
   pieces

salt

sprigs of fresh cilantro,
   to garnish

1 Heat the mustard oil in a large skillet set over a high heat for about 1 minute until it begins to smoke.

2 Add the vegetable oil, reduce the heat and then add the onion and the garlic. Fry the garlic and onion until they are golden.

3 Add the tomato paste, chopped tomatoes, turmeric, ground cumin and cilantro seeds, chili powder, garam masala and wine vinegar to the skillet. Stir the mixture until fragrant.

4 Add the red bell pepper and fava beans and stir for 2 minutes until the pepper is softened. Stir in the chicken, and salt to taste.

5 Simmer gently for 6–8 minutes until the chicken is heated through and the beans are tender.

6 Serve garnished with sprigs of cilantro.

Spiced Apricot Chicken

Spiced chicken legs are partially boned and packed with dried apricot.
A golden, spiced, low-fat yogurt coating keeps the chicken moist.

NUTRITIONAL INFORMATION

Calories	305	Sugars	.......21g
Protein	........15g	Fat	..........8g
Carbohydrate	...45g	Saturates	......1g

10 MINS   40 MINS

SERVES 4

I N G R E D I E N T S

4 large, lean skinless chicken leg quarters

finely grated rind of 1 lemon

1 cup ready-to-eat dried apricots

1 tbsp ground cumin

1 tsp ground turmeric

½ cup low-fat unsweetened yogurt

salt and pepper

TO SERVE

1½ cups brown rice

2 tbsp flaked hazelnuts, toasted

2 tbsp sunflower seeds, toasted

1 Remove any excess fat from the chicken legs. Use a small sharp knife to carefully cut the flesh away from the thigh bone. Scrape the meat away down as far as the knuckle. Grasp the thigh bone firmly and twist it to break it away from the drumstick.

2 Open out the boned part of the chicken and sprinkle with lemon rind and pepper. Pack the dried apricots into each piece of chicken.

3 Fold over to enclose, and secure with cocktail sticks. Mix together the cumin, turmeric, yogurt and salt and pepper, then brush this mixture over the chicken to coat evenly. Place the chicken in an ovenproof dish and bake in a preheated oven, 190°C/375°F/Gas Mark 5, for 35–40 minutes, or until the chicken juices run clear, not pink, when pierced through the thickest part with a skewer.

4 Meanwhile, cook the rice in boiling, lightly salted water until just tender, then drain well. Stir the hazelnuts and sunflower seeds into the rice and serve.

VARIATION

For a change use dried herbs instead of spices to flavor the coating. Use dried oregano, tarragon or rosemary – but remember dried herbs are more powerful than fresh, so you will only need a little.

Ginger Chicken & Corn

Chicken wings and corn in a sticky ginger marinade are designed to be eaten with the fingers – there's no other way!

NUTRITIONAL INFORMATION

Calories ....123 Sugars 3g
Protein ....14g Fat 6g
Carbohydrate ....3g Saturates 1g

🧊 10 MINS   🕐 20 MINS

SERVES 6

I N G R E D I E N T S

3 cobs fresh corn-on-the-cob

12 chicken wings

1 inch piece fresh ginger

6 tbsp lemon juice

4 tsp sunflower oil

1 tbsp golden superfine sugar

jacket potatoes or salad, to serve

1 Remove the husks and silks from the corn. Using a sharp knife, cut each cob into 6 slices.

2 Place the corn in a large bowl with the chicken wings.

3 Peel and grate the ginger root or chop finely. Place in a bowl and add the lemon juice, sunflower oil and golden superfine sugar. Mix together until well combined.

4 Toss the corn and chicken in the ginger mixture to coat evely.

5 Thread the corn and chicken wings alternately on to metal or pre-soaked wooden skewers, to make turning easier.

6 Cook under a preheated moderately hot broiler or grill for 15–20 minutes, basting with the gingery glaze and turning frequently until the corn is golden brown and tender and the chicken is cooked. Serve with jacket potatoes or salad.

COOK'S TIP

Cut off the wing tips before broiling as they burn very easily. Alternatively, you can cover them with small pieces of foil.

Mexican Chicken

Chili, tomatoes and corn are typical ingredients in a Mexican dish. This is a quick and easy meal for unexpected guests.

NUTRITIONAL INFORMATION

Calories	207	Sugars	.........8g
Protein	........18g	Fat	...........9g
Carbohydrate	...13g	Saturates	......2g

5 MINS   35 MINS

SERVES 4

I N G R E D I E N T S

2 tbsp oil

8 chicken drumsticks

1 medium onion, finely chopped

1 tsp chili powder

1 tsp ground cilantro

15 oz can chopped tomatoes

2 tbsp tomato paste

⅔ cup frozen corn-on-the-cob

salt and pepper

TO SERVE

boiled rice

mixed bell pepper salad

1 Heat the oil in a large skillet, add the chicken drumsticks and cook over a medium heat until lightly browned on all sides. Remove from the skillet and set aside.

2 Add the onion to the skillet and cook for 3–4 minutes until soft, then stir in the chili powder and cilantro and cook for a few seconds.

3 Add the chopped tomatoes with their juice and the tomato paste.

4 Return the chicken to the pan and simmer gently for 20 minutes until the chicken is tender and thoroughly cooked. Add the corn-on-the-cob and cook a further 3–4 minutes. Season to taste.

5 Serve with boiled rice and mixed bell pepper salad.

COOK'S TIP

If you dislike the heat of the chilies, just leave them out – the chicken will still taste delicious.

Shrimp Bhuna

This is a fiery recipe with subtle undertones. As the flavor of the shrimp should be noticeable, the spices should not take over.

NUTRITIONAL INFORMATION

Calories 141	Sugars 0.4g	
Protein 19g	Fat 7g	
Carbohydrate 1g	Saturates 1g	

15 MINS   20 MINS

SERVES 4–6

INGREDIENTS

2 dried red chilies, deseeded if liked

3 fresh green chilies, finely chopped

1 tsp ground turmeric

3 garlic cloves, crushed

½ tsp pepper

1 tsp paprika

2 tsp white wine vinegar

½ tsp salt

1 lb 2 oz uncooked peeled king shrimp

3 tbsp oil

1 onion, chopped very finely

¾ cup water

2 tbsp lemon juice

2 tsp garam masala

sprigs of fresh cilantro,
    to garnish

COOK'S TIP

Garam masala should be used sparingly and is generally added to foods towards the end of their cooking time. It is also used sprinkled over cooked meats, vegetables and pulses as a garnish.

1 Combine the chilies, spices, vinegar and salt in a non-metallic bowl. Stir in the shrimp and leave for 10 minutes.

2 Heat the oil in a large skillet or wok, add the onion and fry for 3–4 minutes until soft.

3 Add the shrimp and the contents of the bowl to the pan and stir-fry over a high heat for 2 minutes. Reduce the heat, add the water and boil for 10 minutes, stirring occasionally, until the water is evaporated and the curry is fragrant.

4 Stir in the lemon juice and garam masala then transfer the mixture to a warm serving dish and garnish with fresh cilantro sprigs.

5 Serve garnished with sprigs of fresh cilantro.

Salmon Yakitori

The Japanese sauce used here combines well with salmon, although it is usually served with chicken.

NUTRITIONAL INFORMATION

Calories 247   Sugars 10g
Protein ....19g   Fat 11g
Carbohydrate ...12g   Saturates 2g

20 MINS   15 MINS

SERVES 4

I N G R E D I E N T S

12 oz chunky salmon fillet

8 baby leeks

Y A K I T O R I   S A U C E

5 tbsp light soy sauce

5 tbsp fish stock

2 tbsp superfine sugar

5 tbsp dry white wine

3 tbsp sweet sherry

1 clove garlic, crushed

1 Skin the salmon and cut the flesh into 2 inch chunks. Trim the leeks and cut them into 2 inch lengths.

2 Thread the salmon and leeks alternately on to 8 pre-soaked wooden skewers. Leave to chill in the refrigerator until required.

3 To make the sauce, place all of the ingredients in a small pan and heat gently, stirring, until the sugar has dissolved.

4 Bring to the boil, then reduce the heat and simmer for 2 minutes. Strain the sauce through a fine strainer and leave to cool until it is required.

5 Pour about one-third of the sauce into a small dish and set aside to serve with the kebabs.

6 Brush plenty of the remaining sauce over the skewers and cook directly on the rack.

7 If preferred, place a sheet of oiled kitchen foil on the rack and cook the salmon on that.

8 Grill the salmon and leek kabobs over hot coals for about 10 minutes or until cooked though, turning once.

9 Use a brush to baste frequently during cooking with the remaining sauce in order to prevent the fish and vegetables from drying out. Transfer the kabobs to a large serving platter and serve with a small bowl of the reserved sauce for dipping.

Baked Sea Bass

Sea bass is often paired with subtle oriental flavors. For a special occasion, you may like to bone the fish.

NUTRITIONAL INFORMATION

Calories 140	Sugars 0.1g
Protein 29g	Fat 1g
Carbohydrate . . .0.1g	Saturates 0.2g

🍳 🍳

🥘 10 MINS   🕐 15 MINS

SERVES 4–6

INGREDIENTS

2 sea bass, about 2 lb 4 oz each, cleaned and scaled

2 scallions, green part only, cut into strips

2 inch piece ginger, peeled and cut into strips

2 garlic cloves, unpeeled, crushed lightly

2 tbsp mirin or dry sherry

salt and pepper

TO SERVE

pickled sushi ginger (optional)

soy sauce

1 For each fish lay out a double thickness of foil and oil the top piece well, or lay a piece of silicon paper over the foil.

2 Place the fish in the middle and expose the cavity.

3 Divide the scallion and ginger between each cavity. Put a garlic clove in each cavity.

4 Pour over the mirin or dry sherry. Season the fish well.

5 Close the cavities and lay each fish on its side. Bring over the foil and fold the edges together to seal securely. Fold each end neatly.

6 Cook over a medium grill for 15 minutes, turning once.

7 To serve, remove the foil and cut each fish into 2 or 3 pieces.

8 Serve with the pickled ginger (if using) accompanied by soy sauce.

COOK'S TIP

Fresh sea bass is just as delicious when cooked very simply. Stuff the fish with garlic and chopped herbs, brush with olive oil and bake in the oven.

Curried Crab

If you can buy fresh crab, clean the shell and brush lightly with oil and use as a container for the crab meat.

NUTRITIONAL INFORMATION

Calories	272	Sugars	.........5g
Protein	........27g	Fat	..........16g
Carbohydrate	....5g	Saturates	......2g

5 MINS   15 MINS

SERVES 4

INGREDIENTS

2 tbsp mustard oil

1 tbsp ghee

1 onion, chopped finely

2 inch piece fresh ginger, grated

2 garlic cloves, peeled but left whole

1 tsp ground turmeric

1 tsp salt

1 tsp chili powder

2 fresh green chilies, chopped

1 tsp paprika

½ cup brown crab meat

1½ cups white crab meat

1 cup low-fat unsweetened yogurt

1 tsp garam masala

basmati rice, to serve

fresh cilantro, to garnish

1 Heat the mustard oil in a large, preferably non-stick, skillet, wok or saucepan.

2 When it starts to smoke, add the ghee and onion. Stir for 3 minutes over a medium heat until the onion is soft.

3 Stir in the ginger and whole garlic cloves.

4 Add the turmeric, salt, chili powder, chilies and paprika. Mix thoroughly.

5 Increase the heat and add the crab meat and yogurt. Simmer, stirring occasionally, for 10 minutes until the sauce is thickened slightly.

6 Add garam masala to taste.

7 Serve hot, over plain basmati rice, with the fresh cilantro either chopped or in sprigs.

COOK'S TIP

For an unusual combination of flavors, mix the crab meat with segments of grapefruit in a mayonnaise. Sprinkle with slivers of almonds.

Lemony Monkfish Kabobs

A simple basting sauce is brushed over these tasty kabobs. When served with crusty bread, they make a perfect light meal.

NUTRITIONAL INFORMATION

Calories 191	Sugars 2g
Protein 21g	Fat 11g
Carbohydrate 1g	Saturates 1g

🥄 10 MINS   🕐 15 MINS

SERVES 4

INGREDIENTS

1 lb monkfish tail

2 zucchini

1 lemon

12 cherry tomatoes

8 bay leaves

SAUCE

3 tbsp olive oil

2 tbsp lemon juice

1 tsp chopped, fresh thyme

½ tsp lemon pepper

salt

TO SERVE

green salad leaves

fresh, crusty bread

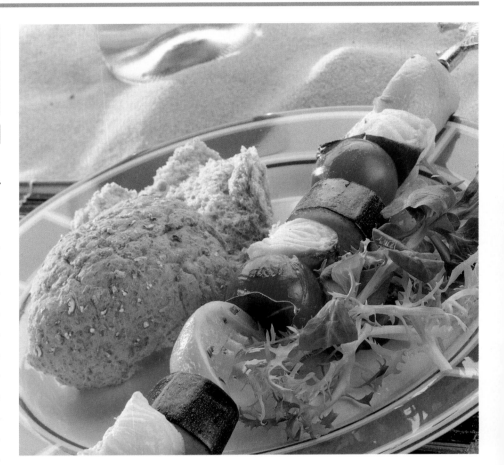

1 Cut the monkfish into 2 inch chunks.

2 Cut the zucchini into thick slices and the lemon into wedges.

3 Thread the monkfish, zucchini, lemon, tomatoes and bay leaves on to 4 skewers.

4 To make the basting sauce, combine the oil, lemon juice, thyme, lemon pepper and salt to taste in a small bowl.

5 Brush the basting sauce liberally all over the fish, lemon, tomatoes and bay leaves on the skewers.

6 Cook the skewers on the grill for about 15 minutes over medium-hot coals, basting them frequently with the sauce, until the fish is cooked through. Transfer the skewers to plates and serve with green salad leaves and wedges of crusty bread.

VARIATION

Use flounder fillets instead of the monkfish, if you prefer. Allow two fillets per person, and skin and cut each fillet lengthways into two. Roll up each piece and thread them on to the skewers.

Fragrant Tuna Steaks

Fresh tuna steaks are very meaty – they have a firm texture, yet the flesh is succulent. Steaks from the belly are best of all.

NUTRITIONAL INFORMATION

Calories	239	Sugars	.......0.1g
Protein	........42g	Fat	..........8g
Carbohydrate	...0.5g	Saturates	......2g

15 MINS   15 MINS

SERVES 4

I N G R E D I E N T S

4 tuna steaks, 6 oz each

½ tsp finely grated lime rind

1 garlic clove, crushed

2 tsp olive oil

1 tsp ground cumin

1 tsp ground cilantro

pepper

1 tbsp lime juice

fresh cilantro, to garnish

TO SERVE

avocado relish (see Cook's Tip, below)

lime wedges

tomato wedges

COOK'S TIP

For the avocado relish, peel and chop a small ripe avocado. Mix in 1 tbsp lime juice, 1 tbsp freshly chopped cilantro, 1 small finely chopped red onion and some chopped fresh mango or tomato. Season to taste.

1 Trim the skin from the tuna steaks, rinse and pat dry on absorbent paper towels.

2 In a small bowl, mix together the lime rind, garlic, olive oil, cumin, ground cilantro and pepper to make a paste.

3 Spread the paste thinly on both sides of the tuna. Heat a non-stick, ridged skillet until hot and press the tuna steaks into the pan to seal them. Lower the heat and cook for 5 minutes. Turn the fish over and cook for a further 4–5 minutes until the fish is cooked through. Drain on paper towels and transfer to a serving plate.

4 Sprinkle the lime juice and chopped cilantro over the fish. Serve with avocado relish (see Cook's Tip), and tomato and lime wedges.

Char-Grilled Mackerel

The sharpness of the apricot glaze complements the oiliness of the fish and has a delicious hint of ginger.

NUTRITIONAL INFORMATION

Calories	343	Sugars	........21g
Protein	........23g	Fat	..........18g
Carbohydrate	...22g	Saturates	......4g

5 MINS   10 MINS

SERVES 4

I N G R E D I E N T S

4 mackerel, about 8 oz each

14 oz can apricots in natural juice

3 tbsp dark muscovado sugar

3 tbsp Worcestershire sauce

3 tbsp soy sauce

2 tbsp tomato paste

1 tsp ground ginger

dash Tabasco sauce

1 clove garlic, crushed (optional)

salt and pepper

1 Clean and gut the mackerel, removing the heads if preferred. Place the fish in a shallow dish.

2 Drain the apricots, reserving the juice. Roughly chop half of the apricots and set aside. Place the remaining apricots in a food processor with the sugar, Worcestershire sauce, soy sauce, tomato paste, ginger, Tabasco sauce and garlic (if using) and process until smooth. Alternatively, chop the apricots and mix with the other ingredients. Season to taste.

3 Pour the sauce over the fish, turning them so that they are well coated on both sides. Leave to chill in the refrigerator until required.

4 Transfer the mackerel to the grill either directly on the rack or on a piece of greased kitchen foil. Grill the mackerel over hot coals for 5–7 minutes, turning once.

5 Spoon any remaining marinade into a saucepan. Add the reserved chopped apricots and about half of the reserved apricot juice and bring to the boil. Reduce the heat and simmer for 2 minutes. Transfer the mackerel to a serving plate and serve with the apricot sauce.

COOK'S TIP

Use a hinged rack if you have one as it will make it much easier to turn the fish during grilling.

Scallop Kabobs

As the scallops are marinated, it is not essential that they are fresh; frozen shellfish are fine for a grill.

NUTRITIONAL INFORMATION

Calories ......182 Sugars 0g
Protein ....29g Fat 7g
Carbohydrate ....0g Saturates 1g

30 MINS   10 MINS

SERVES 4

INGREDIENTS

grated zest and juice of 2 limes

2 tbsp finely chopped lemon grass or 1 tbsp lemon juice

2 garlic cloves, crushed

1 green chili, deseeded and chopped

16 scallops, with corals

2 limes, each cut into 8 segments

2 tbsp sunflower oil

1 tbsp lemon juice

salt and pepper

TO SERVE

1 cup arugula salad

3 cups mixed greens

1 Soak 8 skewers in warm water for at least 10 minutes before you use them to prevent the food from sticking.

2 Combine the lime juice and zest, lemon grass, garlic and chili together in a pestle and mortar or spice grinder to make a paste.

3 Thread 2 scallops on to each of the soaked skewers. Cover the ends with foil to prevent them from burning.

4 Alternate the scallops with the lime segments.

5 Whisk together the oil, lemon juice, salt and pepper to make the dressing.

6 Coat the scallops with the spice paste and place over a medium grill, basting occasionally.

7 Cook for 10 minutes, turning once.

8 Toss the arugula, mixed greens and dressing together well. Put into a serving bowl.

9 Serve the scallops piping hot, 2 kabobs on each plate, with the greens.

Green Fish Curry

This dish has a wonderful fresh, hot, exotic taste resulting from the generous amount of fresh herbs, sharp fresh chilies and coconut milk.

NUTRITIONAL INFORMATION

Calories 223	Sugars 2g
Protein 44g	Fat 5g
Carbohydrate 2g	Saturates 1g

5 MINS   20 MINS

SERVES 4

I N G R E D I E N T S

1 tbsp oil

2 scallions, sliced

1 tsp cumin seeds, ground

2 fresh green chilies, chopped

1 tsp cilantro seeds, ground

4 tbsp chopped fresh cilantro

4 tbsp chopped fresh mint

1 tbsp chopped chives

⅔ cup coconut milk

4 white fish fillets, about 8 oz each

salt and pepper

basmati rice, to serve

1 mint sprig, to garnish

1 Heat the oil in a large skillet or shallow saucepan and add the scallions.

2 Stir-fry the scallions over a medium heat until they are softened but not colored.

3 Stir in the cumin, chilies and ground cilantro, and cook until fragrant.

4 Add the fresh cilantro, mint, chives and coconut milk and season liberally.

5 Carefully place the fish in the pan and poach for 10–15 minutes until the flesh flakes when tested with a fork.

6 Serve the fish fillets in the sauce with the rice. Garnish with a mint sprig.

COOK'S TIP

Never overcook fish – it is surprising how little time it takes compared to meat. It will continue to cook slightly while keeping warm in the oven and while being dished up and brought to the table.

Flounder with Mushrooms

The moist texture of broiled fish is complemented by the texture of the mushrooms.

NUTRITIONAL INFORMATION

Calories	243	Sugars	. . . . .2g
Protein	. . . . .30g	Fat	. . . . .13g
Carbohydrate	. . . .2g	Saturates	. . . . . .3g

10 MINS   20 MINS

SERVES 4

I N G R E D I E N T S

5½ oz white-skinned flounder fillets

2 tbsp lime juice

celery salt and pepper

⅓ cup low-fat spread

2½ cups mixed small mushrooms such as button, oyster, shiitake, chanterelle or morel, sliced or quartered

4 tomatoes, skinned, seeded and chopped

basil leaves, to garnish

mixed salad, to serve

1 Line a broiler rack with baking parchment and place the fish on top.

2 Sprinkle over the lime juice and season with celery salt and pepper.

3 Place under a preheated moderate broiler and cook for 7–8 minutes without turning, until just cooked. Keep warm.

4 Meanwhile, gently melt the low fat spread in a non-stick skillet, add the mushrooms and fry for 4–5 minutes over a low heat until cooked through.

5 Gently heat the tomatoes in a small saucepan.

6 Spoon the mushrooms, with any pan juices, and the tomatoes over the plaice.

7 Garnish the broiled flounder with the basil leaves and serve with a mixed salad.

COOK'S TIP

Mushrooms are ideal in a low-fat diet, as they are packed full of flavor and contain no fat. More 'meaty' types of mushroom, such as crimini, will take slightly longer to cook.

Fish with Black Bean Sauce

Any firm and delicate fish steaks such as salmon or salmon trout can be cooked by the same method.

NUTRITIONAL INFORMATION

Calories ....194 Sugars 0.2g
Protein ....27g Fat 9g
Carbohydrate ....1g Saturates 1g

5 MINS   20 MINS

SERVES 6

INGREDIENTS

1 sea bass, trout or turbot, weighing about
  1 lb 9 oz, cleaned

1 tsp salt

1 tbsp sesame oil

2-3 scallions, cut in half lengthways

1 tbsp light soy sauce

1 tbsp Chinese rice wine or dry sherry

1 tbsp finely shredded fresh ginger

1 tbsp oil

2 tbsp crushed black bean sauce

2 finely shredded scallions

fresh cilantro leaves, to garnish (optional)

lemon slices, to garnish

1 Score both sides of the fish with diagonal cuts at 1 inch intervals. Rub both the inside and outside of the fish with salt and sesame oil.

2 Place the fish on top of the scallions on a heat-proof plate. Blend the soy sauce and wine with the ginger shreds and pour evenly all over the fish.

3 Place the fish on the platter in a very hot steamer (or inside a wok on a rack), cover and steam vigorously for 12-15 minutes.

4 Heat the oil until hot, then blend in the black bean sauce. Remove the fish from the steamer and place on a serving dish.

5 Pour the hot black bean sauce over the whole length of the fish and place the shredded scallions on top. Place the fish on a plate and serve garnished with cilantro leaves (if using) and lemon slices.

COOK'S TIP

If using fish steaks, rub them with the salt and sesame oil, but do not score with a knife. The fish may require less cooking, depending on the thickness of the steaks – test with a skewer after about 8 minutes to check whether they are done.

Scallops with Mushrooms

Scallops have a rich but delicate flavor. When sautéed with mushrooms and bathed in brandy and cream, they make a really special meal.

NUTRITIONAL INFORMATION

Calories	390	Sugars 1g
Protein	........31g	Fat 28g
Carbohydrate	....1g	Saturates 4g

5 MINS   10 MINS

SERVES 2

INGREDIENTS

1 tbsp butter

8 oz shelled queen scallops

1 tbsp olive oil

1¾ oz oyster mushrooms, sliced

1¾ oz shiitake mushrooms, sliced

1 garlic clove, chopped

4 scallions, white and green parts sliced

3 tbsp heavy cream

1 tbsp brandy

salt and pepper

sprigs of fresh dill, to garnish

basmati rice to serve

1 Heat the butter in a heavy-based skillet and fry the scallops for about 1 minute, turning occasionally.

2 Remove the scallops from the skillet with a perforated spoon and keep warm.

3 Add the olive oil to the pan and heat. Add the mushrooms, garlic and scallions and cook for 2 minutes, stirring constantly.

4 Return the scallops to the pan. Add the heavy cream and brandy, stirring well to mix.

5 Season with salt and pepper to taste and heat to warm through.

6 Garnish with fresh dill sprigs and serve with rice.

COOK'S TIP

Scallops, which consist of a large, round white muscle with bright orange roe, are the most delicious seafood in the prettiest of shells. The rounded half of the shell can be used as a dish in which to serve the scallops.

Baked Trout Mexican-Style

Make this dish as hot or as mild as you like by adjusting the amount of red chili. The green chilies are milder and add a pungency to the dish.

NUTRITIONAL INFORMATION

Calories	329	Sugars	.........5g
Protein	........53g	Fat	..........10g
Carbohydrate	....6g	Saturates	......2g

🕑 10 MINS   🕐 30 MINS

SERVES 4

INGREDIENTS

4 trout, 8 oz each

1 small bunch fresh cilantro

4 shallots, shredded finely

1 small yellow bell pepper, deseeded and very finely chopped

1 small red bell pepper, deseeded and very finely chopped

2 green chilies, deseeded and finely chopped

1–2 red chilies, deseeded and finely chopped

1 tbsp lemon juice

1 tbsp white wine vinegar

2 tsp superfine sugar

salt and pepper

fresh cilantro, to garnish

salad leaves, to serve

1 Preheat the oven to 180°C/350°F/Gas Mark 4. Wash the trout and pat dry with paper towels. Season and stuff with cilantro leaves.

2 Place the fish side by side in a shallow ovenproof dish. Sprinkle over the shallots, bell peppers and chilies.

3 Mix together the lemon juice, vinegar and sugar in a bowl. Spoon over the trout and season with salt and pepper. Cover the dish and bake for 30 minutes or until the fish is tender and the flesh is opaque.

4 Remove the the fish with a fish slice and drain. Transfer to warm serving plates and spoon the cooking juices over the fish. Garnish with fresh cilantro and serve with salad and chili bean rice (see Cook's Tip).

COOK'S TIP

For the chili bean rice, cook 1¼ cup long- grain white rice. Drain and rinse a 14 oz can kidney beans and stir into the rice with 1 tsp each of ground cumin and cilantro. Stir in 4 tbsp chopped fresh cilantro and season.

Oriental Vegetable Noodles

This dish has a mild, nutty flavor from the peanut butter and dry-roasted peanuts.

NUTRITIONAL INFORMATION

Calories 193   Sugars 5g
Protein ....7g   Fat 12g
Carbohydrate ...14g   Saturates 2g

10 MINS   15 MINS

SERVES 4

INGREDIENTS

1½ cups green thread noodles or multi-colored spaghetti

1 tsp sesame oil

2 tbsp crunchy peanut butter

2 tbsp light soy sauce

1 tbsp white wine vinegar

1 tsp clear honey

4½ oz mooli, grated

4½ oz/1 large carrot, grated

4½ oz cucumber, shredded finely

1 bunch scallions, shredded finely

1 tbsp dry-roasted peanuts, crushed

TO GARNISH

carrot flowers

scallion tassels

1 Bring a large saucepan of water to the boil, add the noodles or spaghetti and cook according to the packet instructions. Drain well and rinse in cold water. Leave in a bowl of cold water until required.

2 To make the peanut butter sauce, put the sesame oil, peanut butter, soy sauce, vinegar, honey and seasoning into a small screw-top jar. Seal and shake well to mix thoroughly.

3 Drain the noodles or spaghetti well, place in a large serving bowl and mix in half the peanut sauce.

4 Using 2 forks, toss in the mooli, carrot, cucumber and scallions. Sprinkle with crushed peanuts and garnish with carrot flowers and scallion tassels. Serve the noodles with the remaining peanut sauce.

COOK'S TIP

There are many varieties of oriental noodles available from oriental markets and supermarkets. Try rice noodles, which contain very little fat and require little cooking; usually soaking in boiling water is sufficient.

Char-Grilled Vegetables

This medley of bell peppers, zucchini, eggplant and red onion can be served on its own or as an unusual side dish.

NUTRITIONAL INFORMATION

Calories 66	Sugars 7g
Protein 2g	Fat 3g
Carbohydrate 7g	Saturates 0.5g

15 MINS   15 MINS

SERVES 4

INGREDIENTS

1 large red bell pepper

1 large green bell pepper

1 large orange bell pepper

1 large zucchini

4 baby eggplant

2 medium red onions

2 tbsp lemon juice

1 tbsp olive oil

1 garlic clove, crushed

1 tbsp chopped, fresh rosemary or 1 tsp dried rosemary

salt and pepper

TO SERVE

cracked wheat, cooked

tomato and olive relish

1 Halve and deseed the bell peppers and cut into even sized pieces, about 1 inch wide.

2 Trim the zucchini, cut in half lengthways and slice into 1 inch pieces. Place the bell peppers and zucchini in a large bowl.

3 Trim the eggplant and quarter them lengthways. Peel both the onions, then cut each one into 8 even-sized wedges.

4 Add the pieces of eggplant and onions to the bowl containing the wedges of bell peppers and zucchini.

5 In a small bowl, whisk together the lemon juice, olive oil, garlic, rosemary and seasoning.

6 Pour the mixture over the vegetables and stir to coat evenly.

7 Preheat the broiler to medium. Thread the vegetables on to 8 metal or pre-soaked wooden skewers. Arrange the kabobs on the rack and cook for 10–12 minutes, turning frequently until the vegetables are lightly charred and just softened.

8 Drain the vegetable kabobs and serve on a bed of cracked wheat accompanied with a tomato and olive relish.

Spinach & Orange Salad

This is a refreshing and very nutritious salad. Add the dressing just before serving so that the leaves do not become soggy.

NUTRITIONAL INFORMATION

Calories 126	Sugars 10g
Protein 3g	Fat 9g
Carbohydrate ...10g	Saturates 1g

10 MINS   0 MINS

SERVES 4

I N G R E D I E N T S

8 oz baby spinach leaves

2 large oranges

½ red onion

D R E S S I N G

3 tbsp extra virgin olive oil

2 tbsp freshly squeezed orange juice

2 tsp lemon juice

1 tsp clear honey

½ tsp wholegrain mustard

salt and pepper

1 Wash the spinach leaves under cold running water and then dry them thoroughly on paper towels. Remove any tough stalks and tear the larger leaves into smaller pieces.

2 Slice the top and bottom off each orange with a sharp knife, then remove the peel. Carefully slice between the membranes of the orange to remove the segments. Reserve any juices for the salad dressing.

3 Using a sharp knife, finely chop the onion.

4 Mix together the salad leaves and orange segments and arrange in a serving dish.

5 Scatter the chopped onion over the salad.

6 To make the dressing, whisk together the olive oil, orange juice, lemon juice, honey, mustard and salt and pepper to taste in a small bowl.

7 Pour the dressing over the salad just before serving. Toss the salad well to coat the leaves with the dressing.

VARIATION
Use a mixture of spinach and watercress leaves, if you prefer a slightly more peppery flavor.

Mixed Leaf Salad

Make this green, leafy salad from as many varieties of salad leaves and flowers as you can find to give an unusual effect.

NUTRITIONAL INFORMATION

Calories 51	Sugars 0.1g	
Protein 0.1g	Fat 6g	
Carbohydrate 1g	Saturates 1g	

🍰 5 MINS   🕐 0 MINS

SERVES 4

I N G R E D I E N T S

½ head chicory

½ head oak leaf lettuce or quattro stagione

few leaves of radicchio

1 head endive

2½ cup arugula leaves

few sprigs fresh basil or flat-leaf parsley

6 tbsp French dressing

flowers of your choice (see Cook's Tip)

1 Tear the chicory, oak leaf lettuce and radicchio into manageable pieces.

2 Place the greens into a large serving bowl, or individual bowls if you prefer.

3 Cut the endive into diagonal slices and add to the bowl with the arugula leaves, basil or parsley.

4 Pour the dressing over the salad and toss thoroughly. Scatter a mixture of flowers over the top.

COOK'S TIP

Violas, rock geraniums, nasturtiums, chive flowers and pot marigolds add vibrant colors and a sweet flavor to any salad. Use it as a centrepiece at a dinner party, or to liven up a simple everyday meal.

Root Vegetable Salad

This salad of grated vegetables is perfect for a light starter. The peppery flavors of the mooli and radishes are refreshingly pungent.

NUTRITIONAL INFORMATION

Calories 132   Sugars 9g
Protein ....4g   Fat 8g
Carbohydrate ...12g   Saturates 1g

🥗 20 MINS   🕐 0 MINS

SERVES 4

INGREDIENTS

12 oz carrots

8 oz mooli (white radish)

4 oz radishes

12 oz celery root

1 tbsp orange juice

2 sticks celery with leaves, washed and trimmed

3½ oz assorted greens

1 oz walnuts, chopped

DRESSING

1 tbsp walnut oil

1 tbsp white wine vinegar

1 tsp wholegrain mustard

½ tsp finely grated orange rind

1 tsp celery seeds

salt and pepper

1 Peel and coarsely grate or very finely shred the carrots, mooli (white radish) and radishes. Set aside in separate bowls.

2 Peel and coarsely grate or finely shred the celery root and mix with the orange juice.

3 Remove the celery leaves and reserve. Finely chop the celery sticks.

4 Divide the greens among 4 serving plates and arrange the vegetables in small piles on top. Set aside while you make the dressing.

5 Mix all of the dressing ingredients together and season well. Drizzle a little over each salad.

6 Shred the reserved celery leaves and sprinkle over the salad with the chopped walnuts.

COOK'S TIP

Also known as Chinese white radish and daikon, mooli resembles a large white parsnip. It has crisp, slightly pungent flesh, which can be eaten raw or cooked. It is a useful ingredient in stir-fries.

Coleslaw

Home-made coleslaw tastes far superior to any that you can buy. If you make it in advance, add the sunflower seeds just before serving.

NUTRITIONAL INFORMATION

Calories 224	Sugars 8g
Protein 3g	Fat 20g
Carbohydrate 8g	Saturates 3g

🍳 10 MINS   🕓 5 MINS

SERVES 4

INGREDIENTS

⅔ cup low-fat mayonnaise

⅔ cup low-fat unsweetened yogurt

dash of Tabasco sauce

1 medium head white cabbage

4 carrots

1 green bell pepper

2 tbsp sunflower seeds

salt and pepper

1 To make the dressing, combine the mayonnaise, yogurt, Tabasco sauce and salt and pepper to taste in a small bowl. Leave to chill until required.

2 Cut the cabbage in half and then into quarters. Remove and discard the tough centre stalk. Shred the cabbage leaves finely. Wash the leaves and dry them thoroughly.

3 Peel the carrots and shred using a food processor or mandolin. Alternatively, coarsely grate the carrot.

4 Quarter and deseed the bell pepper and cut the flesh into thin strips.

5 Combine the vegetables in a large mixing bowl and toss to mix. Pour over the dressing and toss until the

vegetables are well coated. Leave to chill in the refrigerator until required.

6 Just before serving, place the sunflower seeds on a cookie sheet and toast them in the oven or under the broiler until golden brown. Transfer the salad to a large serving dish, scatter with sunflower seeds and serve.

VARIATION

For a slightly different taste, add one or more of the following ingredients to the coleslaw: raisins, grapes, grated apple, chopped walnuts, cubes of cheese or roasted peanuts.

Quick Bean Salad

This attractive-looking salad served with meat from the grill makes a delicious light meal in summer.

NUTRITIONAL INFORMATION

Calories 139   Sugars 5g
Protein ....8g   Fat 3g
Carbohydrate ...21g   Saturates 0.4g

10 MINS   0 MINS

SERVES 4

INGREDIENTS

14 oz can garbanzo beans

4 carrots

1 bunch scallions

1 medium cucumber

½ tsp salt

½ tsp pepper

3 tbsp lemon juice

1 red bell pepper

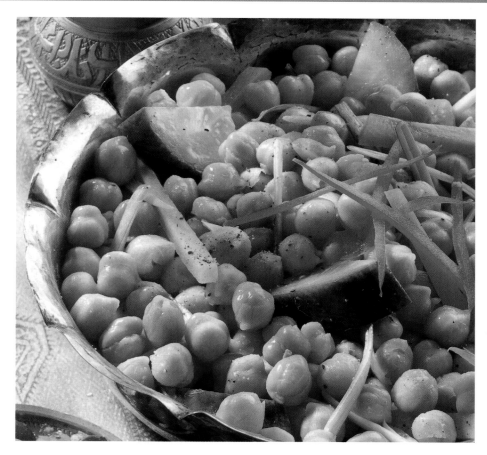

1 Drain the garbanzo beans and place in a salad bowl.

2 Using a sharp knife, peel and slice the carrots.

3 Cut the scallions into small pieces.

4 Cut the cucumber into thick quarters.

5 Add the carrots, scallions and cucumber to the garbanzo beans and mix. Season with the salt and pepper and sprinkle with the lemon juice.

6 Toss the salad ingredients together gently using 2 serving spoons.

7 Using a sharp knife, slice the red bell pepper thinly.

8 Arrange the slices of red bell pepper on top of the garbanzo bean salad.

9 Serve the salad immediately or leave to chill in the fridge and serve when required.

COOK'S TIP

Using canned garbanzo beans rather than the dried ones speeds up the cooking time.

Waldorf Chicken Salad

This colorful and healthy dish is a variation of a classic salad. You can use a selection of mixed salad leaves, if preferred.

NUTRITIONAL INFORMATION

Calories 471	Sugars 19g	
Protein 38g	Fat 27g	
Carbohydrate ...20g	Saturates 4g	

30 MINS   0 MINS

SERVES 4

INGREDIENTS

1 lb 2 oz red apples, diced

3 tbsp fresh lemon juice

⅔ cup low-fat mayonnaise

1 head of celery

4 shallots, sliced

1 garlic clove, crushed

¾ cup walnuts, chopped

1 lb 2 oz lean cooked chicken, cubed

1 romaine lettuce

pepper

sliced apple and walnuts, to garnish

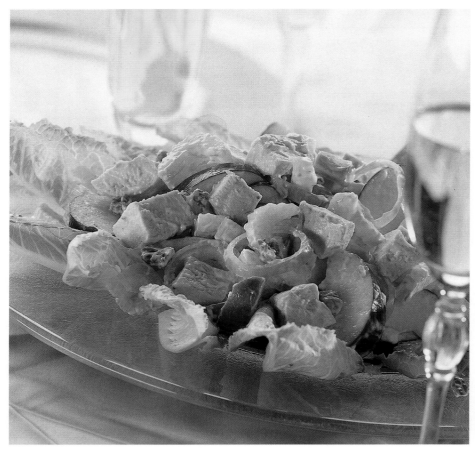

1 Place the apples in a bowl with the lemon juice and 1 tablespoon of mayonnaise. Leave for 40 minutes or until required.

2 Slice the celery very thinly. Add the celery with the shallots, garlic and walnuts to the apple, mix and then add the remaining mayonnaise and blend thoroughly.

3 Add the chicken and mix with the other ingredients.

4 Line a glass salad bowl or serving dish with the lettuce.

5 Pile the chicken salad into the centre, sprinkle with pepper and garnish with apple slices and walnuts.

VARIATION

Instead of the shallots, use scallions for a milder flavor. Trim the scallions and slice finely.

Salad with Garlic Dressing

This is a very quick and refreshing salad using a whole range of colorful ingredients which make it look as good as it tastes.

NUTRITIONAL INFORMATION

Calories . . . . .82 Sugars 5g
Protein . . . . .2g Fat 6g
Carbohydrate . . . .5g Saturates 1g

10 MINS   0 MINS

SERVES 4

INGREDIENTS

2¾ oz cucumber, cut into sticks

6 scallions, halved

2 tomatoes, seeded and cut into eight

1 yellow bell pepper, cut into strips

2 celery stalks, cut into strips

4 radishes, quartered

2¾ oz arugula

1 tbsp chopped mint, to serve

DRESSING

2 tbsp lemon juice

1 garlic clove, crushed

⅔ cup low-fat unsweetened yogurt

2 tbsp olive oil

salt and pepper

1 To make the salad, mix the cucumber, scallions, tomatoes, bell pepper, celery, radishes and arugula together in a large serving bowl.

2 To make the dressing, stir the lemon juice, garlic, unsweetened yogurt and olive oil together.

3 Season well with salt and pepper to taste.

4 Spoon the dressing over the salad and toss to mix. Sprinkle the salad with chopped mint and serve.

COOK'S TIP

Arugula has a distinct warm, peppery flavor which is ideal in green salads. If arugula is unavailable, corn salad makes a good substitute.

Coronation Salad

This dish is based on Coronation Chicken which was invented to celebrate Queen Victoria's coronation as a symbol of Anglo-Indian links.

NUTRITIONAL INFORMATION

Calories .... 236 Sugars 24g
Protein .... 7g Fat 5g
Carbohydrate ...43g Saturates 1g

25 MINS   0 MINS

SERVES 4

INGREDIENTS

1 red bell pepper

⅓ cup golden raisins

1 celery stalk, sliced

¾ cup corn

1 Granny Smith apple, diced

1 cup white seedless grapes, washed and halved

1½ cups cooked basmati rice

½ cup cooked, peeled shrimp (optional)

1 romaine lettuce, washed and drained

1 tsp paprika to garnish

DRESSING

4 tbsp low-fat mayonnaise

2 tsp mild curry powder

1 tsp lemon juice

1 tsp paprika

pinch of salt

1 Deseed and chop the red bell pepper.

2 Combine the golden raisins, red bell pepper, celery, corn, apple and grapes in a large bowl. Stir in the rice, and shrimp, if using.

3 For the dressing, put the mayonnaise, curry powder, lemon juice, paprika and salt into a small bowl and mix well.

4 Pour the dressing over the salad and gently mix until evenly coated.

5 Line the serving plate with romaine lettuce leaves and spoon on the salad. Sprinkle over the paprika and serve.

COOK'S TIP

Mayonnaise can be bought in varying thicknesses, from the type that you spoon out of the jar to the pouring variety. If you need to thin down mayonnaise for a dressing, simply add water little by little until the desired consistency is reached.

Minted Fennel Salad

This is a very refreshing salad. The subtle licorice flavor of fennel combines well with the cucumber and mint.

NUTRITIONAL INFORMATION

Calories 90   Sugars 7g
Protein . . . . .4g   Fat 5g
Carbohydrate . . . .7g   Saturates 1g

25 MINS   0 MINS

SERVES 4

I N G R E D I E N T S

1 bulb fennel

2 small oranges

1 small or ½ large cucumber

1 tbsp chopped mint

1 tbsp virgin olive oil

2 eggs, cooked

1 Using a sharp knife, trim the outer leaves from the fennel. Slice the fennel bulb thinly into a bowl of water and then sprinkle with lemon juice (see Cook's Tip).

2 Grate the rind of the oranges over a bowl. Using a sharp knife, pare away the orange peel, then segment the orange by carefully slicing between each line of pith. Do this over the bowl in order to retain the juice.

3 Using a sharp knife, cut the cucumber into ½ inch rounds and then cut each round into quarters.

4 Add the cucumber to the fennel and orange mixture together with the mint.

5 Pour the olive oil over the fennel and cucumber salad and toss well.

6 Peel and quarter the eggs and use these to decorate the top of the salad. Serve immediately.

COOK'S TIP

Fennel will discolor if it is left for any length of time without a dressing. To prevent any discoloration, place it in a bowl of water and sprinkle with lemon juice.

Moroccan Couscous Salad

Couscous is a type of semolina made from durum wheat. It is wonderful in salads as it readily takes up the flavor of the dressing.

NUTRITIONAL INFORMATION

Calories	...195	Sugars	...15g
Protein	...8g	Fat	...2g
Carbohydrate	...40g	Saturates	...0.3g

15 MINS 15 MINS

SERVES 6

INGREDIENTS

2 cups couscous

1 bunch scallions, trimmed and chopped finely

1 small green bell pepper, cored, deseeded, and chopped

4 inch piece cucumber, chopped

7 oz can garbanzo beans, rinsed and drained

⅔ cup golden raisins

2 oranges

salt and pepper

lettuce leaves, to serve

sprigs of fresh mint, to garnish

DRESSING

finely grated rind of 1 orange

1 tbsp chopped fresh mint

⅔ cup low-fat unsweetened yogurt

VARIATION

As an alternative, use cracked wheat instead of the couscous. Rinse thoroughly until the water runs clear, then soak in boiling water for 1 hour. Strain if necessary.

1 Put the couscous into a bowl and cover with boiling water. Leave it to soak for about 15 minutes to swell the grains, then stir with a fork to separate them.

2 Add the scallions, green bell pepper, cucumber, garbanzo beans and golden raisins to the couscous, stirring to combine. Season well with salt and pepper.

3 To make the dressing, mix the orange rind, mint, and yogurt. Pour over the couscous mixture and stir well.

4 Using a sharp serrated knife, remove the peel and pith from the oranges. Cut the flesh into segments, removing all the membrane.

5 Arrange the greens on serving plates. Divide the couscous mixture between the plates and arrange the orange segments on top.

6 Garnish with sprigs of fresh mint and serve.

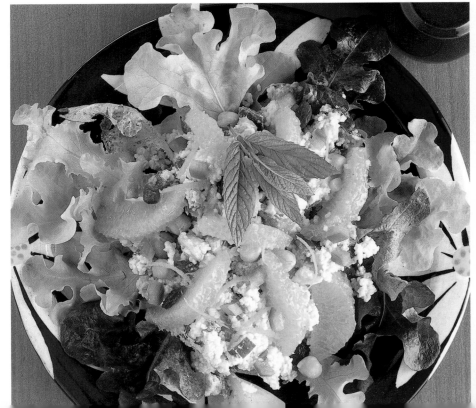

Mussel Salad

A colorful combination of cooked mussels tossed together with char-grilled red bell peppers and salad leaves in a lemon dressing.

40 MINS   10 MINS

SERVES 4

INGREDIENTS

2 large red bell peppers

12 oz cooked shelled mussels, thawed if frozen

1 head of radicchio

1 oz arugula leaves

8 cooked New Zealand mussels in their shells

TO SERVE

lemon wedges

crusty bread

DRESSING

1 tbsp olive oil

1 tbsp lemon juice

1 tsp finely grated lemon rind

2 tsp clear honey

1 tsp French mustard

1 tbsp snipped fresh chives

salt and pepper

1 Preheat the broiler to hot. Halve and deseed the bell peppers and place them skin-side up on the rack.

2 Cook for 8–10 minutes until the skin is charred and blistered and the flesh is soft. Leave to cool for 10 minutes, then peel off the skin.

3 Slice the bell pepper flesh into thin strips and place in a bowl. Gently mix in the shelled mussels and set aside until required.

4 To make the dressing, mix all of the ingredients until well blended.

5 Mix into the bell pepper and mussel mixture until coated.

6 Remove the central core of the radicchio and shred the leaves. Place in a serving bowl with the arugula leaves and toss together.

7 Pile the mussel mixture into the centre of the leaves and arrange the large mussels in their shells around the edge of the dish. Serve with lemon wedges and crusty bread.

Sweet & Sour Fruit

This mixture of fresh and canned fruit, which has a sweet and sour flavor, is very cooling, especially in the summer.

NUTRITIONAL INFORMATION

Calories 240	Sugars 58g	
Protein 2g	Fat 0.4g	
Carbohydrate ...60g	Saturates 0g	

5 MINS   0 MINS

SERVES 4

INGREDIENTS

14 oz can mixed fruit cocktail

14 oz can guavas

2 large bananas

3 apples (optional)

1 tsp ground black pepper

1 tsp salt

½ tsp ground ginger

2 tbsp lemon juice

fresh mint leaves, to garnish

1 Drain the can of mixed fruit cocktail and place the fruit in a deep mixing bowl.

2 Mix the drained fruit cocktail with the guavas and their syrup so that the fruit is well coated.

3 Peel the bananas and cut into thick slices.

4 Peel the apples (optional) and cut into dice.

5 Add the fresh fruit to the bowl containing the canned fruit and mix together.

6 Add the ground black pepper, salt and ginger and stir to mix. Add the lemon juice to prevent the banana and apple from turning brown and mix again.

7 Serve the sweet and sour fruit as a snack garnished with a few fresh mint leaves.

COOK'S TIP

Guavas are tropical fruits with a powerful, exotic smell. You may find fresh guavas in specialist shops and large supermarkets, but the canned variety is more widely available. Surprisingly, they have a higher vitamin C content than many citrus fruits.

Carrot & Orange Salad

A crunchy and colorful, sweet and savory dish which would also make an excellent appetizer.

NUTRITIONAL INFORMATION

Calories . . . . . . .194 Sugars 25g
Protein . . . . .6g Fat 8g
Carbohydrate . . .26g Saturates 1g

20 MINS   0 MINS

SERVES 4

I N G R E D I E N T S

1 lb 2 oz celery root

2 tbsp orange juice

4 carrots, sliced finely

2 celery stalks, chopped finely

1 cup celery leaves

4 oranges

¼ cup walnut pieces

D R E S S I N G

1 tbsp walnut oil

½ tsp grated orange rind

3 tbsp orange juice

1 tbsp white wine vinegar

1 tsp clear honey

salt and pepper

1 Trim and peel the celery root and slice or grate finely into a bowl. Add the orange juice and toss together.

2 Mix in the carrots, celery and celery leaves. Cover and chill while preparing the oranges.

3 Slice off the tops and bottoms from the oranges. Using a sharp knife, slice off the skin, taking the pith away at the same time. Cut out the orange flesh by slicing along the side of the membranes dividing the segments. Gently mix the segments into the celery root mixture.

4 To make the dressing, place all the ingredients in a small screw-top jar. Seal and shake well to mix.

5 Pile the vegetable mixture on to a plate. Sprinkle over the walnut pieces and serve with the dressing.

COOK'S TIP

Celery root is a variety of celery with a bulbous, knobbly root. It has a rough, light brown skin and creamy white flesh and is delicious raw or cooked.

Tomato Salsa

This salad is used extensively in Mexican cooking and served as a dip or a relish, and is eaten as an accompaniment to almost any dish.

NUTRITIONAL INFORMATION

Calories	10	Sugars	. . . . .2g
Protein	. . . . .0.4g	Fat	. . . . .0.1g
Carbohydrate	. . . .2g	Saturates	. . . . . .0g

10 MINS   0 MINS

SERVES 4

INGREDIENTS

4 ripe red tomatoes

1 medium red onion or 6 scallions

1–2 garlic cloves, crushed (optional)

2 tbsp chopped fresh cilantro

½ red or green chili (optional)

finely grated rind of ½–1 lemon or lime

1–2 tbsp lemon or lime juice

pepper

1 Chop the tomatoes fairly finely and evenly, and put into a bowl. They must be firm and a good strong red color for the best results, but if preferred, they may be peeled by placing them in boiling water for about 20 seconds and then plunging into cold water. The skins should then slip off easily when they are nicked with a knife.

2 Peel and slice the red onion thinly, or trim the scallions and cut into thin slanting slices; add to the tomatoes with the garlic and cilantro and mix lightly.

3 Remove the seeds from the red or green chili (if using) chop the flesh very finely and add to the salad. Treat the chilies with care; do not touch your eyes or face after handling them until you have washed your hands thoroughly. Chili juices can burn.

4 Add the lemon or lime rind and juice to the salsa, and mix well. Transfer to a serving bowl and sprinkle with pepper.

COOK'S TIP

If you don't like the distinctive flavor of fresh cilantro, you can replace it with flat-leaf parsley instead.

Eggplant Curry

This is a rich vegetable dish, ideal served with a tandoori chicken and naan bread. It is also delicious served as a vegetarian dish with rice.

NUTRITIONAL INFORMATION

Calories	73	Sugars 6g
Protein	.........3g	Fat 4g
Carbohydrate	....6g	Saturates 1g

15 MINS   15 MINS

SERVES 6

INGREDIENTS

2 whole eggplants

1 cup low-fat unsweetened yogurt

2 cardamom pods

½ tsp ground turmeric

1 dried red chili

½ tsp cilantro seeds

½ tsp ground black pepper

1 tsp garam masala

1 clove

2 tbsp sunflower oil

1 onion, sliced lengthways

2 garlic cloves, crushed

1 tbsp grated fresh ginger

6 ripe tomatoes, peeled, deseeded and quartered

fresh cilantro, to garnish

1 If you have a gas cooker, roast the 2 eggplants over a naked flame, turning frequently, until charred and black all over This should take about 5 minutes. Peel under running cold water. Cut off the stem end and discard.

2 Put the peeled eggplant into a large bowl and mash lightly with a fork. Stir in the yogurt.

3 Grind together the cardamom pods, turmeric, red chili, cilantro seeds, black pepper, garam masala and clove in a large pestle and mortar or spice grinder.

4 Heat the oil in a wok or heavy skillet over a moderate heat and cook the onion, garlic and fresh ginger until soft. Add the tomatoes and ground spices, and stir well.

5 Add the eggplant mixture to the pan and stir well. Cook for 5 minutes over a gentle heat, stirring constantly, until all the flavors are combined, and some of the liquid has evaporated.

6 Serve the eggplant immediately, garnished with cilantro.

Raitas

Raitas are very easy to prepare, very versatile and have a cooling effect which will be appreciated if you are serving hot, spicy dishes.

NUTRITIONAL INFORMATION

Calories 33	Sugars 5g
Protein 3g	Fat 0.4g
Carbohydrate 5g	Saturates 0.3g

10 MINS   5 MINS

SERVES 4

INGREDIENTS

MINT RAITA

¾ cup low-fat unsweetened yogurt

4 tbsp water

1 small onion, finely chopped

½ tsp mint sauce

½ tsp salt

3 fresh mint leaves, to garnish

CUCUMBER RAITA

8 oz cucumber

1 medium onion

½ tsp salt

½ tsp mint sauce

1¼ cups low-fat unsweetened yogurt

⅔ cup water

fresh mint leaves, to garnish

EGGPLANT RAITA

1 medium eggplant

1 tsp salt

1 small onion, finely chopped

2 green chilies, finely chopped

¾ cup low-fat unsweetened yogurt

3 tbsp water

1 To make the mint raita, place the yogurt in a bowl and whisk with a fork. Gradually whisk in the water. Add the onion, mint sauce and salt and blend together. Garnish with mint leaves.

2 To make the cucumber raita, peel and slice the cucumber. Chop the onion finely. Place the cucumber and onion in a large bowl, then add the salt and the mint sauce. Add the yogurt and the water and place the mixture in a liquidizer and blend well. Serve garnished with mint leaves.

3 To make the eggplant raita, remove the top end of the eggplant and chop the rest into small pieces. Boil in a pan of water until soft, then drain and mash. Add the salt, onion and green chilies, mixing well. Whip the yogurt with the water and add to the mixture and mix thoroughly.

Spicy Cauliflower

This is a perfectly delicious way to serve cauliflower. It can be enjoyed as a salad or at a picnic, or as a side dish to a main meal.

5 MINS   15 MINS

SERVES 4

INGREDIENTS

1 lb 2 oz cauliflower, cut into florets

1 tbsp sunflower oil

1 garlic clove

½ tsp turmeric

1 tsp cumin seeds, ground

1 tsp cilantro seeds, ground

1 tsp yellow mustard seeds

12 scallions, sliced finely

salt and pepper

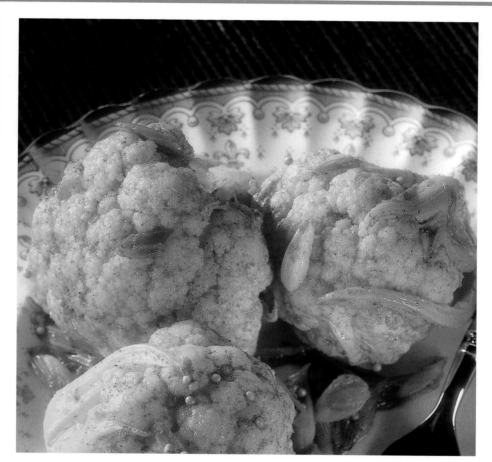

1 Blanch the cauliflower in boiling water, drain and set aside. Cauliflower holds a lot of water, which tends to make it over-soft, so turn the florets upside-down at this stage and you will end up with a crisper result.

COOK'S TIP

For a special occasion this dish looks great made with baby cauliflowers instead of florets. Peel off most of the outer leaves, leaving a few for decoration, and blanch the baby cauliflowers whole for 4 minutes and drain. Continue as in step 2.

2 Heat the oil gently in a large, heavy skillet or wok. Add the garlic clove, turmeric, ground cumin, ground cilantro and mustard seeds. Stir well and cover the pan.

3 When you hear the mustard seeds popping, add the scallions and stir. Cook for 2 minutes, stirring constantly, to soften them a little. Season to taste.

4 Add the cauliflower and stir for 3–4 minutes until coated completely with the spices and thoroughly heated.

5 Remove the garlic clove and serve immediately.

Sesame Seed Chutney

This chutney is delicious served with spiced rice dishes, and also makes an unusual filling to spread in sandwiches.

NUTRITIONAL INFORMATION

Calories 120	Sugars 0g	
Protein 4g	Fat 12g	
Carbohydrate ...0.2g	Saturates 2g	

🕙 10 MINS   ⏱ 5 MINS

SERVES 4

I N G R E D I E N T S

8 tbsp sesame seeds

2 tbsp water

½ bunch fresh cilantro

3 fresh green chilies, chopped

1 tsp salt

2 tsp lemon juice

chopped red chili, to garnish

1 Place the sesame seeds in a large, heavy-based saucepan and dry roast them. Set the sesame seeds aside to cool.

2 Once cooled, place the sesame seeds in a food processor or pestle and mortar and grind well to form a fine powder.

3 Add the water to the sesame seeds and mix thoroughly to form a smooth paste.

4 Using a sharp knife, finely chop the cilantro.

5 Add the chilies and cilantro to the sesame seed paste and grind once again.

6 Add the salt and lemon juice to the mixture and grind once again.

7 Remove the mixture from the food processor or pestle and mortar and transfer to a serving dish. Garnish with red chili and serve.

COOK'S TIP

Dry roasting brings out the flavor of dried spices and takes just a few minutes. You will be able to tell when the spices are ready because of the wonderful fragrance that develops. Stir the spices constantly to ensure that they do not burn.

Colcannon

This is an old Irish recipe, usually served with a piece of bacon, but it is equally delicious with chicken or fish.

NUTRITIONAL INFORMATION

Calories 102   Sugars 4g
Protein . . . . .4g   Fat 4g
Carbohydrate . . .14g   Saturates 2g

5 MINS   35 MINS

SERVES 4

INGREDIENTS

8 oz green cabbage, shredded

⅓ cup skimmed milk

8 oz mealy potatoes,
  diced

1 large leek, chopped

pinch of grated nutmeg

1 tbsp butter, melted

salt and pepper

1 Bring a large saucepan of salted water to the boil, add the shredded cabbage and cook for 7–10 minutes. Drain thoroughly and set aside.

2 Meanwhile, in a separate saucepan, bring the milk to the boil and add the potatoes and leek. Reduce the heat and simmer for 15–20 minutes or until they are cooked through.

COOK'S TIP

There are many different varieties of cabbage, which produce hearts at varying times of year, so you can be sure of being able to make this delicious cabbage dish all year round.

3 Stir in the grated nutmeg and mash the potatoes and leeks together.

4 Add the drained cabbage to the potatoes and mix well.

5 Spoon the potato and cabbage mixture into a serving dish, making a

hollow in the centre with the back of a spoon.

6 Pour the melted butter into the hollow and serve the colcannon immediately.

Thai Fragrant Coconut Rice

Basmati rice is cooked with creamed coconut, lemon grass, fresh ginger and spices to make a wonderfully aromatic, fluffy rice.

NUTRITIONAL INFORMATION

Calories	258	Sugars	.......0.4g
Protein	.........5g	Fat	..........6g
Carbohydrate	...51g	Saturates	......4g

5 MINS   20 MINS

SERVES 4–6

I N G R E D I E N T S

1 inch piece fresh ginger, peeled
   and sliced

2 cloves

1 piece lemon grass, bruised and
   halved

2 tsp ground nutmeg

1 cinnamon stick

1 bay leaf

2 small thin strips lime zest

1 tsp salt

1 oz creamed coconut, chopped

2½ cups water

1¾ cups basmati rice

ground pepper

1 Place the ginger, cloves, lemon grass, nutmeg, cinnamon stick, bay leaf, lime zest, salt, creamed coconut and water in a large, heavy-based pan and bring slowly to the boil.

2 Add the rice, stir well, then cover and simmer, over a very gentle heat, for about 15 minutes or until all the liquid has been absorbed and the rice is tender but still has a bite to it.

3 Alternatively, bring the rice to the boil then cover tightly and turn off the heat. Leave for 20–25 minutes before removing the lid – the rice will be perfectly cooked.

4 Remove from the heat, add pepper to taste, then fluff up the rice with a fork.

5 Remove the large pieces of spices before serving.

COOK'S TIP

When using a whole stem of lemon grass (rather than chopped lemon grass), beat it well to bruise it so that the flavor is fully released. Lemon zest or a pared piece of lemon peel can be used instead.

Mixed Fruit Brûlées

Traditionally a rich mixture made with cream, this fruit-based version is just as tempting using unsweetened yogurt as a topping.

NUTRITIONAL INFORMATION

Calories	165	Sugars	........21g
Protein	.........5g	Fat	..........7g
Carbohydrate	...21g	Saturates	......5g

🕐 5 MINS   🕐 5 MINS

SERVES 4

I N G R E D I E N T S

1 lb prepared assorted summer fruits (such as strawberries, raspberries, blackcurrants, redcurrants and cherries), thawed if frozen

¾ cup half-fat heavy cream alternative

¾ cup low-fat unsweetened yogurt

1 tsp vanilla extract

4 tbsp brown crystal sugar

1   Divide the prepared strawberries, raspberries, blackcurrants, redcurrants and cherries evenly among 4 small heatproof custard pots.

2   Mix together the half-fat cream alternative, unsweetened yogurt and vanilla extract until well combined.

3   Generously spoon the mixture over the fruit in the custard pots, to cover the fruit completely.

4   Preheat the broiler to hot.

5   Top each serving with 1 tbsp brown crystal sugar and broil the desserts for 2–3 minutes, until the sugar melts and begins to caramelize. Leave to stand for a couple of minutes before serving.

COOK'S TIP

Look out for half-fat creams, in light and heavy varieties. They are good substitutes for occasional use. Alternatively, in this recipe, omit the cream and double the quantity of yogurt for a lower fat version.

Chocolate & Pineapple Cake

Decorated with thick yogurt and canned pineapple, this is a low-fat cake, but it is by no means lacking in flavor.

NUTRITIONAL INFORMATION

Calories	...199	Sugars	...19g
Protein	...5g	Fat	...9g
Carbohydrate	...28g	Saturates	...3g

🍰 10 MINS   🕐 25 MINS

SERVES 9

INGREDIENTS

⅔ cup low-fat spread

4½ oz superfine sugar

¾ cup self-rising flour, strained

3 tbsp unsweetened cocoa, strained

1½ tsp baking powder

2 eggs

8 oz can pineapple pieces in natural juice

½ cup low-fat thick unsweetened yogurt

about 1 tbsp confectioners' sugar

grated chocolate, to decorate

1 Lightly grease a 8 inch square cake pan.

2 Place the low-fat spread, superfine sugar, flour, unsweetened cocoa, baking powder and eggs in a large mixing bowl. Beat with a wooden spoon or electric hand whisk until smooth.

3 Pour the cake mixture into the prepared pan and level the surface. Bake in a preheated oven, 190°C/325°F/Gas Mark 5, for 20-25 minutes or until springy to the touch. Leave to cool slightly in the pan before

transferring to a wire rack to cool completely.

4 Drain the pineapple, chop the pineapple pieces and drain again. Reserve a little pineapple for decoration, then stir the rest into the yogurt and sweeten to taste with confectioners' sugar.

5 Spread the pineapple and yogurt mixture over the cake and decorate with the reserved pineapple pieces. Sprinkle with the grated chocolate.

Tropical Fruit Fool

Fruit fools are always popular, and this light, tangy version will be no exception. Use your favorite fruits in this recipe if you prefer.

NUTRITIONAL INFORMATION

Calories 149	Sugars 25g	
Protein 6g	Fat 0.4g	
Carbohydrate ...32g	Saturates 0.2g	

35 MINS   0 MINS

SERVES 4

INGREDIENTS

1 medium ripe mango

2 kiwi fruit

1 medium banana

2 tbsp lime juice

½ tsp finely grated lime rind, plus extra to decorate

2 medium egg whites

15 oz can low-fat custard

½ tsp vanilla extract

2 granadillas

1 To peel the mango, slice either side of the smooth, flat central stone. Roughly chop the flesh and blend the fruit in a food processor or blender until smooth. Alternatively, mash with a fork.

VARIATION

Other tropical fruits to try include paw-paw purée, with chopped pineapple and dates or pomegranate seeds to decorate. Or make a summer fruit fool by using strawberry purée, topped with raspberries and blackberries and cherries.

2 Peel the kiwi fruit, chop the flesh into small pieces and place in a bowl. Peel and chop the banana and add to the bowl. Toss all of the fruit in the lime juice and rind and mix well.

3 In a grease-free bowl, whisk the egg whites until stiff and then gently fold in the custard and vanilla extract until thoroughly mixed.

4 In 4 tall glasses, alternately layer the chopped fruit, mango purée and custard mixture, finishing with the custard on top. Leave to chill in the refrigerator for 20 minutes.

5 Halve the granadillas, scoop out the seeds and spoon the granadillas over the fruit fools. Decorate each serving with the extra lime rind and serve.

This is a Parragon Publishing Book
This edition published in 2003

Parragon Publishing
Queen Street House
4 Queen Street
Bath BA1 1HE, UK

ISBN: 1-40540-877-4

Printed in China

NOTE

This book uses metric and imperial measurements. Follow the same units
of measurement throughout; do not mix metric and imperial.
All spoon measurements are level: teaspoons are assumed to be 5 ml, and
tablespoons are assumed to be 15 ml. Unless otherwise stated,
milk is assumed to be full fat, eggs and individual vegetables such as potatoes
are medium, and pepper is freshly ground black pepper.

The nutritional information provided for each recipe is per serving or per person.
Optional ingredients, variations or serving suggestions have
not been included in the calculations. The times given for each recipe are an approximate
guide only because the preparation times may differ according to the techniques used by
different people and the cooking times may vary as a result of the type of oven used.

Recipes using raw or very lightly cooked eggs should be
avoided by infants, the elderly, pregnant women, convalescents,
and anyone suffering from an illness.

The publisher would like to thank
Steamer Trading Cookshop, Lewes, East Sussex, for the kind loan of props.